ME VS. MYSELF

THE ANXIETY GUY TELLS ALL

Me VS Myself
Copyright © 2018 by Dennis Simsek

All rights reserved. No part of this publication may be reproduced, distributed, or transmitted in any form or by any means, including photocopying, recording, or other electronic or mechanical methods, without the prior written permission of the author, except in the case of brief quotations embodied in critical reviews and certain other non-commercial uses permitted by copyright law.

Tellwell Talent
www.tellwell.ca

ISBN
978-0-2288-0023-1 (Hardcover)
978-0-2288-0022-4 (Paperback)
978-0-2288-0024-8 (eBook)

DEDICATED TO MY FAMILY, WHO STAYED BY MY SIDE DURING THE ROLLER-COASTER RIDE THAT IS ANXIETY, AND TO THE MILLIONS OUT THERE WHO ARE READY FOR CHANGE. REMEMBER, YOU ARE MORE THAN ANXIETY!

INTRODUCTION

My name is Dennis Simsek and I want to thank you for picking up The Anxiety Guy Tells All—a book that dives deep into my two passions: playing tennis and ending anxiety.

This story is about what life was like for me at the bottom of the ladder in professional tennis. Sleeping on beaches, finding the cheapest food, and using glue to put my deteriorating tennis shoes back together were just some of the challenges I ran into. Yes, I was often completely broke. In addition to the battles on the tennis court—with some outrageous and disrespectful individuals—I had a debilitating anxiety disorder, and all of that led me on a journey most people wouldn't dare take on naturally.

Anxiety disorders are the most common mental illness in the U.S., affecting some 40 million adults aged 18 and older. If you're one of those people, you will likely notice similarities in your own life to the events and experiences that I'll be sharing here with you. I'll explain the things I did that added to my fears and high anxiety levels, as well as the things that worked for me, and I'll outline how I eventually ended my anxiety disorder completely and naturally.

I hope this book will inspire you to take the steps necessary to transform your life. It will take patience and perseverance to follow my methods, which are based around Cognitive Behavioural Therapy (CBT) and Neuro Linguistic Programming (NLP), but *you will* come through this better in the end.

CHAPTER 1

WHO IS THE ANXIETY GUY?

I KNOW YOU'RE FEELING ANXIOUS, BUT THERE'S ALSO A PART OF YOU THAT'S A BADASS!

Even though my dad had told me that life was like playing a tennis match uphill with no end in sight, I wasn't ready for the roller coaster ride that awaited me. Living with generalized anxiety disorder (GAD), panic disorder, hypochondria, and depression, while trying to make a living in the sport of tennis was exhausting. It was like trying to win a shouting match with John McEnroe over a line call while running down Rafael Nadal's blistering groundstrokes all day.

I grew up in an athletic family, and I was told not to reinvent the wheel when it came to trying new tennis shots on the court, but to follow the pros, and to copy what they had did to be successful. Not surprisingly, this works in other areas of life as well. I discovered that the key to overcoming mental health issues naturally is to follow someone who has recovered, and mimic what they did.

Our Emotions Create our Experiences

By living in constant fear—whether it's about being judged by others, leaving the house (agoraphobia), or driving—people with anxiety create a state of anxious and unfulfilling emotions. These emotions include regret, unworthiness, overwhelm, and hopelessness, just to name a few.

In order to make a change, the most important thing you need to do is to make a decision. Make a decision now that you will not go through one more day of just coping with anxiety. How? You need to see the end result in your mind first. If you don't have a clear picture of the way you want your life to be, you won't know where you're going, and you won't recognize it once you've achieved your goals.

Action Item: What do you want your life to look like?

- Right now, sit quietly and picture in your mind's eye how you want your life to be once you've overcome GAD and health anxiety.
- How do you see yourself at work with your co-workers?
- How do you see yourself at home with your family?
- What kind of energy do you want to have?
- See it. Feel it. And **believe it will happen**. Hold on to that feeling, and those images. **Your mind is your inner GPS system, and it needs your guidance.**

The Six Human Needs

We meet our six human needs (certainty, uncertainty, love and connection, growth, significance, and contribution) in either positive or negative ways. Boy, did I find ways to meet them in negative ways. I wondered why I couldn't just push through my GAD and release myself from the prison of anxiety that I felt trapped in? The reason was that the mind will only accept a new belief when tremendous amounts of emotion and repetition accompany the new thought pattern.

My mind had been programmed, from a young age, to fight everything. Nothing was good enough, and I focused on potential threats, which fuelled the anxiety. This thinking pattern is very common—focusing on what's wrong, rather than looking for what's right.

A Day in My Life

I dealt with GAD, health anxiety, and panic disorder for 6 long years. I started each morning by waking up and checking to see if there was pain in my chest or if my heart was pounding…it was. I staggered to the bathroom, holding on to something due to feeling unsteady, and noticed in the mirror how awful I looked and wondered what my fiancée saw in me. Then I'd start worrying about how I was going to get through the day, and how much I dreaded seeing everyone I'd have to come into contact with.

Even a simple walk in the park could set off anxiety. If someone looked at me a second too long I'd wonder if they were judging me for something like my clothes, or the way I walked.

That's what the mind does: **It sorts for information in the outside world that connects with how we see ourselves on the inside.** This is called the Reticular Activating System and it's located in our subconscious minds. It's the reason why anxious people get more anxious, depressed people get more depressed, and lucky people get more lucky.

Let's use the example of shopping at a mall. A sales clerk asks, "Can I help you?" A non-anxious person knows the clerk is just doing her job. I, on the other hand, would say, "No thank you, I'm just looking," but thinking, "Why am I being pressured to buy something? If I needed her help I'd ask for it! Geez I hate pushy people!" This usually started a cycle of anxiety and panic for me that included coughing, spitting, cracking my knuckles, or nail biting.

Quickly, my thoughts became negative and fearful, which manifested as physical symptoms—extreme dizziness, heart palpitations, or migraines. This led me to flee the mall or park as soon as possible (the fight, freeze, or flight response). Then came the shortness of breath, followed by feeling like I was dying—the worst feeling I've ever felt, and one I wouldn't wish on my worst enemy. Then someone would call the emergency, landing me in a bed next to people I was starting to get to know quite well. The cycle seemed unending.

Not only did certain people or places trigger panicky reactions, things like food and beverages set off my anxiety. To a person who doesn't suffer from GAD or panic disorder, having a beer is relaxing, but for me, it brought up memories of past times when I wound up in the ER or shaking in fear. As a tennis coach, it was difficult for me to say no to a client who wanted to share a beer after a lesson or a group that invited me to their weekend tennis social. Not wanting to be rude, I would attend these get-togethers and have a few beers.

Once in a while people would ask me if I was OK after I drank one beer. Next thing I knew, the physical sensations kicked in and I felt dizzy. It didn't take long for my mind to associate alcohol to feelings of panic, regardless of how many drinks I had.

Our subconscious minds record our emotional reactions to each experience. That's why panic became my default reaction in this case.

The spiralling continued. One day I was walking around, feeling exhausted even though I had slept 8 hours and had eaten a healthy breakfast, thinking that something was terribly wrong. Why did the world seem like a dream? I was experiencing depersonalization and derealization—the sense that the world had become less real and lacking in significance. I dragged myself around in a daze, almost like being drugged, with an off-balance feeling.

That day I knew that I had to make some drastic changes in every part of my life. But even though I deeply wanted to change, there was a part of me that didn't want change. GAD and health anxiety had become my comfort zone. I thought that if I gave up worrying, I would lose control. If I lost control, that would lead to the ultimate fear—death.

It reached the point where my mind was in fight, flight, or freeze mode from the minute I woke up to the minute I went to sleep. On top of the physical manifestations of anxiety, I was also stuck in a dreamlike trance.

My life was affected in every way, and people noticed. Someone would say something important, but it didn't register in my mind because I was too busy keeping tabs on my symptoms and checking in with how I was feeling inside.

For years this was my daily struggle. I had nights when I would cry and ask, "Why me?" and surf the Web trying to find solutions to battle the evil thing that had taken over my life.

I hadn't always been this way. In my early 20s I was free from negative thoughts. If someone stepped on my foot on the bus, I could brush it off in a few seconds and move on. But by my late 20s, if the same thing happened, it would ruin my whole day (bruised foot, blood clot, or cancer I thought!).

Understanding Anxiety

Our ancestors needed the fight, flight, or freeze response in case of danger, such as being chased by an animal. They needed to be quick and react in an instant. The mind needed to recognize a threat and the body needed to be ready to do battle or run.

But in the modern world, this response can be confusing. My mind and body were reacting as if there was a sabre-toothed tiger around every corner. Why couldn't I understand and accept that these physical sensations were just my body's way of preparing itself to fight? Doctors kept reassuring me that I was completely healthy, and that I had nothing to worry about, so why the cycle? Because I continued to fear the unknown, my mind kept saying "this is it" or "this time it will end me" or "maybe the doctor missed something."

Looking for a New Life

During my 6-year struggle, I read a lot of self-help books that described so-called "miracle techniques" to get rid of anxiety in an instant. I also had a cabinet full of remedies recommended by doctors and websites. One important thing I realized was that none of that information was written by someone who had gone through high levels of anxiety first-hand, and for as long as I had.

Thankfully, I eventually found my way out of health anxiety, GAD and panic. I made a complete turnaround and have regained control over my thoughts and my life, and have stopped fear from rushing in and overtaking me.

CHAPTER 2

THE EARLY YEARS

IT'S NEVER TOO LATE TO BECOME THE
PERSON YOU TRULY WANT TO BE.

I started playing tennis at the age of 4. My dad wanted me to become the next Andre Agassi. My days started with practice at 6 a.m., followed by home schooling, then more tennis in the afternoon, followed by fitness. As a junior tennis star growing up in Vancouver, British Columbia, Canada, I learned early on about the pressure to win, and I found it difficult to play my best game while my dad was staring at me from the sidelines, ready to verbally give it to me if I lost a point, or, god forbid, a match!

When I was 9, I had my first tennis tournament. I ran off the court with a proud smile and my mom hugged me. But my dad reprimanded me, and then on the way home, he told me to throw the trophy out of the car because he didn't think I had given 110% on the court. When we got home, I was sent to my room with the door slammed behind me. As I look back on my childhood, I realize how early my anxiety started.

Me VS Myself

"Why are You so Slow?"

Hadi gidiyoruz! That means, "Get up, let's go!" in Turkish. I knew the phrase well, as my dad yelled it nearly every day just before we hopped on our bikes. The bike ride took us about 40 minutes to circle around the seawall in Vancouver. This was no joyride; it was agonizing.

He'd speed up in front of me, and if I lagged behind, he'd give me an earful. If I stopped during the ride, he'd make me do the whole thing again.

That was asking a lot from a 12-year-old. It wasn't fun father-and-son outing; no, this was part of my training on the road to tennis glory. I hated it.

"Everyone in Holland bikes," he'd say.

"Yes, dad, but not in this way," I thought.

Sometimes I had to ride over the long Lions Gate Bridge, but the steep uphill and scary downhill led me to crash my bike on the metal guards rails a few times.

"Suck it up," or "don't look down," he'd say as we crossed the bridge. I wondered if he really cared about me or if he was just using me to reach his dream of sitting in the players' box watching his son on the grass courts at Wimbledon.

My legs always burned at the end of the bike ride, but my dad would say, "Never show anyone that you are tired." I got pretty good at that after a while.

I got good at never showing my feelings at all.

Constant Training

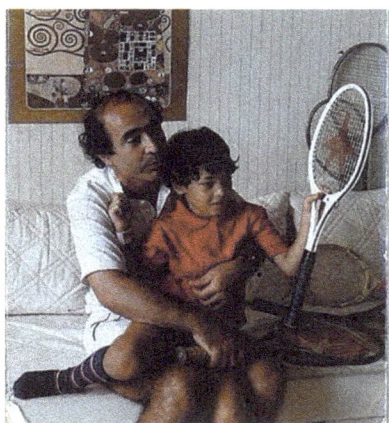

I didn't have much fun between the ages of 8 and 16 because of all this training. The bike ride was usually followed by tennis practice. If the courts were wet from rain, we used our jackets, sweaters, and socks to dry the court. The training was relentless. My dad would find stronger adults to play against me during practice. He rarely played with me; he was usually on the sidelines urging me to "fight" or "fight harder."

Training continued at home—my whole mindset was supposed to be on the game. Even at night, if I wasn't watching a tennis match and learning how to "do it properly," I was reading articles from the latest tennis magazine.

My coaches told me to keep a tennis journal and write down my results, whether I was at practice or a real match. When I had a rare break in the action, I'd write my reviews of what was working and what needed more work.

I wanted to run away from home because I felt like I was living in a prison.

Between the ages of 0-10 our brains are the most neuroplastic, which means we are the most available to suggestion from others. We see something; it becomes us. We hear something; it becomes us. During my youth, I had conditioned a negative way of thinking and looking at life.

At a Crossroads

When I was 13, my dad thought I needed a new training environment in order for me to make it to the top of the tennis ladder. The National

Me VS Myself

Training Centre in Toronto recognized my talent in the Canadian tournaments, and offered me a discounted rate to train with the best coaches. My dad decided to move us to Toronto. The day we left, we squeezed as much as we could into our old Cadillac, and began our five-day drive east.

On the third night, my dad wanted to put in a few extra hours on the road. Visibility was challenging because of the snow and darkness, and the roads were slick. We were driving high up in the mountains and there were no side rails on the road. I held my mom tight as we chugged up and down the mountains. The weather quickly got worse.

Finally, I yelled, "Stop!" I couldn't take much more of the drive and I wanted my dad to pull over, but he kept driving. And then...it happened.

As the slight downhill of the road started to take shape, we hit a patch of ice and our car went into a 360-degree spin. Luckily we were on a straight stretch of road; otherwise, we would have gone over the cliff. The car spun three times and, surprisingly, stayed on the road. To this day, I still remember my mother screaming as we came to a stop, with the front of the car just overlooking the cliff. My dad had pulled the emergency brake. If he had instinctively pushed on the brake pedal, we would have all been dead.

After the car stopped, my dad gave us both a huge hug and we all cried. I finally felt the love I'd been searching for, and it took a near-death experience to get him to show it.

After a few minutes of consoling each other, he backed the car away from the cliff, and put on the hazard lights, hoping that a driver would stop and help us. After about an hour, a car came by. My dad told the driver what had happened, and he led us to a nearby motel.

We could have easily been killed in those mountains that night. When I looked back on that experience as an adult, I realized how my brain's amygdala had held on to the emotions of that almost-tragic night.

For me, that event manifested as a fear of heights and Cadillacs. Every time I saw a large-size car, especially a Cadillac, I became anxious and sensations ran through my body. I realized that until I changed the meaning of what I feared, I'd continue to experience the same feelings and catastrophic thoughts.

My mind was reacting as if this was a life or death experience, and I had to flood myself with the thing I feared, get comfortable with the sensations as I dialogued with my anxious mind, and create new images in my mind in order to change that.

Toronto Training

Once we arrived in Toronto, we moved into our new home near York University where my training facility was located; my new high school was nearby. It was a "sports school," where young athletes were allowed to leave early due to their strict training schedules, but the requirements were quite steep. I was lucky to get in.

I started training the day after we moved in. My dad told me to run to the tennis club while he drove. It took me 45 minutes. Once there, I got into my shorts and shirt, and met some of the coaches and players—they were incredibly friendly and welcoming. I felt comfortable around them, but I already missed Vancouver.

As group practice got underway, I noticed a cute girl, named Tina, who was part of our practice that day (can you say puppy love?). We were put through some challenging drills and match play as they compared me to the rest of the juniors. The coaches all agreed that my potential to be great was there, but they said my dad had to step aside. He was told he could drop me off and pick me up at the tennis club, and that was all.

The coaches wanted me to focus on improving my game, and not on meeting the expectations of my dad. (They had heard about some of his antics from people in Vancouver.) I was thrilled, but my dad didn't like the idea one bit. They also told him that his behaviour might hurt me into my adult years.

As our practice came to an end, it was fitness time. One of the top Canadian fitness trainers was in charge, and I was put through endurance drills, strength drills, foot speed drills, and mental toughness drills. The amount of fitness we did was more than I'd ever done before; it made the bike ride around the seawall look like a cakewalk.

A few weeks went by and everything was going well. I was enjoying training, making friends at school, and getting to know Tina at tennis practice. Then the time came to play in the annual Orange Bowl Championships in Florida, which brought together the top under-14 players to compete for the title. Some of the Top 10 players in the world have competed in, and won, the Orange Bowl, so this was a huge honour and opportunity for me.

In the first round I was drawn up against Spanish up-and-comer Juan Carlos Ferrero, who would later go on to become the #1 tennis player in the world. At the time I didn't know much about Juan Carlos, but the people around me acted like he was a god. I felt incredible pressure and anticipatory anxiety.

Action Item: Anticipatory anxiety is a product of Negative Automatic Thoughts (NATS) and is a story based around little, or no, evidence.

- Recognize when you begin to anticipate a possible catastrophic outcome. Begin turning your focus to the opposite of that possibility.

- Example of anticipatory anxiety: A fire truck just drove by. My house is on fire!

- Opposite replacement: The chances of that happening are highly unlikely, and even if it did, I have insurance.

Anticipatory anxiety is caused by the part of the brain called the cerebral cortex. It reacts to thoughts, and then turns those thoughts into images. Working on changing your thought patterns will change your beliefs, which in turn will change your emotions and the images you unconsciously create.

As I was walked onto the court I saw Juan Carlos getting last-minute pointers from his three coaches—yes, three coaches! I thought this guy must be really good, and he was. The first set went flying by and Juan Carlos won 6-2. I could see my dad pacing back and forth in the stands pumping his fist at me.

The second set was going head-to-head and the score was 3-3. Then we tied 4-4, and then 5-5. At 6-6 we played a tiebreaker, which means the first one to reach 7 points wins the set. It was my serve; a long exchange ensued, ending with a shot from Juan Carlos that clipped the top of the net and landed on my side of the court. I wanted to curse the world. The next points went by quickly as his confidence rose and mine dropped.

If I had won, it would have led to endorsement deals and financial help. But it wasn't meant to be. Afterward, my dad let me know how poorly I had started the match and how I could have done so much better. At this point, he was yelling. Two security guards escorted him off, but he said he would speak to me at the hotel. I felt sad and embarrassed.

Later that night, while sitting by the hotel pool, I saw Tina. I didn't even know she had made the trip. She came over and sat next to me, and we started chatting. All the while, in the back of my mind, I was thinking of my dad.

As Tina and I got closer, I leaned in for my first "real" kiss. I didn't know what I was doing—whether I should keep my lips sealed or open my mouth—but she didn't care. She said goodnight and went up to her room. At that moment I felt like a regular kid with no restraints. But then I noticed a set of eyes behind me. It was my dad, about 5 metres away. My legs started shaking. He approached me, and with a shrug, said, "Go to sleep now." I knew he had seen me kissing Tina. I did what I was told, and went to bed.

The next day I heard from one of the parents that my dad had flown back to Toronto. I knew that he was unhappy with me, but I was relieved. My coaches told me that they would ban him from watching me play tennis, not only in practice, but in tournaments as well.

I called my mom, and she confirmed that my dad was back in Toronto and he wasn't happy. I told her about my first kiss and how well I did in my Orange Bowl match. She was happy for me.

"Everything is going to be fine," she said, even though I could hear my dad yelling in the background, "Get back on track!"

CHAPTER 3

THE WORLD THROUGH AN OVERLY ANXIOUS MIND

**ALL THE THINGS THAT KEEP US
STUCK HAVE BEEN LEARNED.**

When I was 17, my parents separated; my dad told my mom goodbye and left for his home country of Turkey. That meant that for the first time in my life, he wasn't running the show. It was time for me to try to turn pro.

I had just graduated from high school and had no real job skills. I did, however, have a few tennis racquets that I had bought at garage sales, an open mind, and a willingness to do whatever I had to do to build the life I wanted.

I wasn't very social at this point, and that made it difficult for me to find hitting partners to train with. So I did the next best thing—I used tennis backboards. I perfected my volleys at train stations while waiting for the train (someone actually tipped me once) and used the side of a grocery store while waiting for a bus. I even used the backboard of a basketball net late at night, with the lights on, and did my regular 3,000 repetitions of stroke practice.

This persistence and drive was fuelled by the vision I had for my life. Even when I felt extremely lonely and defeated, there was a voice in my head encouraging me to keep going.

Problems, Problems

Most people think they shouldn't have any problems, but problems are a sign that you're alive, and we all deal with them on a daily basis. Back then, I didn't handle my problems very well, and they definitely affected me on the court.

For example, if I was one game away from winning a match and then lost that game, I immediately got down on myself—sometimes even throwing my racquet into places racquets shouldn't go (there are still many of my racquets stuck in trees around the world). It was no surprise that I brought the same negative routines to my life off the court. The over-worrying cycle led me to being overly anxious, and eventually, clinically depressed.

Jimmy Connors—one of the best-ever tennis players—was an inspiration to me growing up. He once said, "I didn't lose the tennis match, I just simply ran out of time." Connors believed that tennis was about solving problems: If he had more time, he'd be able to solve the problem he faced on the court and eventually be victorious. What a great way to look at a tennis match, and life as a whole. When we make progress our main goal, we can say we gave it our all. This will help us leave a legacy, and inspire others.

The professional tennis tour taught me how important it is to be strong—physically, mentally, technically, and tactically—to be a good problem solver. Just like in our daily lives, taking time to strengthen physically (through exercise, sports, working out); mentally (using rational thinking, reframing the past, meditating); technically (doing activities correctly); and tactically (balancing everything out properly throughout the day) can give us the momentum required to make good decisions, solve problems, and keep fear and worry away.

My First Panic Attack

The day had started like any other day; I felt sensitized but it wasn't overwhelming, however, as I ruminated over thoughts about how the day might go, my body reacted first to the anticipatory anxiety. This began a downward spiral towards a full-blown panic attack. The next thing I knew, my greatest fears—hyperventilation and dizziness—came true.

When the panic attack struck, I truly thought I was dying. It felt like an out-of-body experience. I remember saying a prayer and thanking the world for a life filled with adventure, and having been given the gift of what my dad called my "golden arm," because of my tennis skills.

The panicky feelings eventually subsided, but I was left dazed and confused about what had happened. GAD instantly set in, and from that day forward, I found my world becoming smaller and smaller. The free and fearless tennis warrior that I had once been was now just a memory. I wasn't free—I had health anxiety, GAD, and panic disorder.

I now saw the world, other people, and myself, as being dangerous. The world seemed dangerous because I had no sense of balance or self-control. People were dangerous because I feared their judgement and becoming embarrassed. I was dangerous because a thought or emotion could trigger a response that would instantly shoot physical sensations through my body. Welcome to the crazy cycle of curiosity (asking yourself, "What is this feeling?"), what-if thinking, and coping/reassurance seeking.

The label of having panic disorder and anxiety was something I started to carry with me. It became my identity and my mind reminded me of it all the time, no matter what I was doing. That's because the brain sorts for information in the outside world that connects to how we feel, and the way we see ourselves (the aforementioned Reticular Activating System at work). I noticed every poster that said, "Hey, have you gotten your heart checked lately?" I connected worry to safety, worry to maintaining good health, and worry to love and connection from other people—it was all a lie.

My anxious identity would say things like, "When you play tennis, remember not to put too much effort into it, otherwise you might have another panic attack, or worse, a heart attack!" I was subconsciously sabotaging myself.

From the minute I woke up each morning, I couldn't wait to go back to sleep again so I didn't have to face my new anxious identity.

Every waking minute was met with the two words that consumed me, "**What if?**" What if I experience hyperventilation again? What if people think I'm crazy? What if I can't play a tennis match tomorrow because my anxiety symptoms will be too much for me? What if? What if? What if?

I'd like to eliminate these two words from every anxious person's vocabulary. They add fuel to the fear-and-anxiety cycle because it puts the mind into the future. It dictates everything from how you're feeling, to what your future experiences will be.

During some of the tennis tournaments I played in, I remember having such fearful "what if" thoughts of potential panic, that it stopped me from even stepping onto the court.

Action Item: Your emotions are a signal.

- Your emotions are showing you that either you're in line with what you want (fulfillment, joy, happiness) or out of line with what you want (sad, anxious, fearful). This exercise is to recognize when you begin to overreact to an emotion (and think that it's real), when in fact it's only an interpretation that your anxious mind has created.

- Think of a recent experience when you overreacted. How could you have handled it differently knowing that you have self-control over your negative emotions?

Music Changed My Brain Circuitry

One thing I loved to do was deejay. It was a great release for me, because for a few hours my thoughts were focused on syncing music for people to dance to, instead of indulging in my usual negative thinking. It gave me so much freedom; I became hooked on that feeling—no thoughts, just pure positive energy all around me. Eventually I started my own mobile deejay business and did weddings, parties, and pretty much any event.

Music can be a trigger for positive or negative experiences. House Music was one of the biggest triggers to my anxiety, but shortly after buying my deejay equipment, I decided to spin some. I think House Music was a trigger because of its fast tempo. It reminded me of being at the peak of panic when everything is moving out of control.

One night, there was a song playing loudly from one turntable while another song was about to be mixed in on the other one, and I was listening to it through my headphones. I felt my body go into the fight or flight mode, and my thoughts went into a frenzy, but this time I didn't run. I withstood the feeling of losing control and stayed where I was.

For some reason I yelled at the top of my lungs, "Go to hell anxiety!" I was scared, but I kept going, feeling horrible and awesome at the same time.

After another 20 minutes of mixing music and yelling, I was exhausted, but felt surprisingly alive. For the first time, I had some relief from my physical sensations. The negative thoughts were still there, but I was too tired to care anymore.

Dating With Panic

Dating wasn't easy for me during this time. Although on the outside I looked somewhat confident, on the inside my anxiety was about a 9 out of 10. For instance, a blind date would usually start off well, but once we sat down I could feel the blood rushing to my face, as I grew more nervous. Then I'd feel pressured to have a drink, and I knew it was only a matter of time before the physical sensations—shortness of breath and extreme dizziness—would kick in. I had three options at this point.

1. Suck it up and have some drinks, which would trigger unbearable anxiety for the next few days, and probably send me to the ER again.
2. Hang in there, and take a few bathroom breaks to throw cold water on my blushing face.
3. Fake an emergency and leave the restaurant.

The most positive choice would be #2, but I chose #1 because alcohol provides temporary relief from high levels of anxiety. After four beers, I felt like the person I wanted to be—outgoing, confident, and fearless. A few hours later, my invincibility wore off and I started thinking about how difficult the next couple of days would be. This set off the cycle of worry and fear, which turned into physical sensations, followed by confusion, and more fear.

A Ray of Hope

Two years into my GAD and health anxiety, I met the love of my life, Robyn Olsen. I was 28 and she was 23. We ran into each other at a tennis party in Calgary, Alberta. I had lost a match earlier that day, by a matter of a few points, and had already consumed one too many when I noticed her. Boy, did she look good; no wonder she was surrounded by a group of guys. I looked over at Robyn's friend, Jen, who wasn't my type, but was my ticket to finding out more about Robyn.

Brave and extremely intoxicated, I began asking Jen questions about Robyn. Is she single? Does she have kids? What does she do? The questions poured out of my mouth like I was hitting service returns with my eyes closed, and I smiled from ear to ear. I couldn't wait to talk to Robyn, and to show her what I was made of, even though I was extremely drunk.

Later, as I stood near the dance floor, Jen and Robyn walked up to me. She simply said, "Hi, I'm Robyn."

"Helllloooo, I'm Dennis," I replied in a very creepy and skanky voice. I knew my superpowers were leaving me, and Robyn was my kryptonite. A million voices went off in my head, and none of them could save me from this frozen feeling (damn you, amygdala, why now!).

Jen quickly jumped in to save me from myself and began telling Robyn about me. I still couldn't talk because I was afraid of saying the wrong thing. The situation went from bad to worse, and I said, "I'm sorry, I have to go now."

I scattered down the road to catch a cab, feeling defeated. As I stepped into the taxi, Jen handed me a note with Robyn's phone number on it. I grabbed it and got in. As the cab drove off, I started worrying about my next move. When should I call Robyn? What would she think? Then I passed out in the car.

Little did I know at the time that a few years later Robyn and I would be engaged. I must have done something right during the next few dates. She would later tell me how sweet I looked trying to get words out of my mouth on the night we met.

Hitting Rock Bottom

By the age of 29, serious depression kicked in, and things went from bad to worse. As unbelievable as this sounds, I tried to keep the depression going rather than working towards ending it. I looked for pity from my fiancée and friends, and I got along with people who saw the world as a dark, cruel place, just like I did. Of course, the energy I was giving off attracted more of those people and negative experiences into my life, and I hated who I was becoming.

I got drawn into things that provided temporary relief, such as video games, junk food, shopping (even though I didn't love what I bought, I just had to buy something, and quickly get out of there), and for a short time, marijuana.

During the "dark ages," as I refer to that time, my mom and Robyn suggested I see a therapist, so I did. I coughed up $175 per session and bought a package of six sessions—one a week. During every session, my therapist dug deep to get to the root of my anxiety, to see if there was still some hatred towards my dad (which there was), or anything else that happened during my childhood that I was still carrying around.

I thought therapy might be the way to get my life back on track, but I didn't feel like we were dealing with the experience I was currently having. We kept going over the past; she tried to convince me that the past was what was causing all of my grief now.

The therapist couldn't relate to what I was going through; she kept referring to her textbook for answers to my questions. I stuck with therapy until the end of the sixth session, but by that time I was disappointed, and I left therapy even more depressed. I thought I couldn't make any lasting change, and I hadn't been given any solid tools to put me on the right track.

I realized that the only way to turn this ship around was to completely dedicate myself to a brand-new healthy lifestyle and stick to it religiously. I also needed to do things that would make a lasting change in my life.

The Turning Point

My therapist told me that I could never **end** my GAD, health anxiety, and panic issues—I could only *cope*, and hope that I have more good days than bad. I am here to tell you that that is FALSE!

I am proof that complete recovery from an anxiety disorder is possible and can be done naturally. If you're tired of simply coping with fear, Begin Your Recovery Today. The End The Anxiety Program is the #1 CBT-based program to overcome health anxiety and GAD.

The turning point for me—in conquering high levels of anxiety and bringing them down to normal—was recognizing the thinking that led me down the dark tunnel. The pattern of how I initially reacted to a panicky situation was something I worked on retraining for months before I saw improvement.

I lived by these words: **Every anxious moment is an opportunity to practice a new approach**. This means I could see my thoughts, emotions, and past behaviours differently. I was determined to catch myself whenever I fell into a negative cycle, and to replace those thoughts with new, more-realistic and positive ones.

A Fresh Start

I began monitoring which situations, and times of day, triggered my negative thoughts. I got a notebook and named it A Fresh Start. This was my anxiety book. Whenever I had a recurring negative thought, I'd write it down, and note what time it happened. For example, when I woke up in the morning, I thought, "I hate my job, I hate my job, I hate my job!" I wrote down that thought, and the time of day, and from there I worked on ways to make my job more enjoyable. By noticing this thought, I was able to take action towards making myself feel better.

In the weeks that followed, the thought, "I hate my job" turned into "I'm enjoying my job, because now I'm giving better lessons and feeling better physically." This step tested my patience and awareness, but by sticking to it, I noticed big changes in my thought process that positively affected my energy levels. Eventually this became my normal way of thinking.

Another important thing that worked well for me was planning. As difficult as it was for me at first, as soon as I started planning out my days and weeks, and doing mental exercises on paper, I started to see noticeable changes in the way I approached situations. If you come up with a well-thought-out plan, and stick to it, you're going to have success conquering the unrealistic thoughts that overwhelm you, as well as the feelings that can be so exhausting and difficult to deal with.

In order to completely overcome GAD and panic, it is vital to reprogram the mind. As you reprogram your mind, situations that used to drive you crazy can be shrugged off and replaced with thoughts like, "This problem isn't worth getting worked up over. I'm going to turn my focus this way instead," and the anxiety cycle is broken before it starts. This is a result of three important realizations:

   A. **A thought is just a thought**. We have 60,000 thoughts a day. Why focus on the fear-based ones so much?

   B. **A feeling is just a feeling**. It's simply a wrong interpretation of an event, that's all, it's not life threatening

   C. **You are more than anxiety**! The anxious thoughts, feelings, and behaviours you do are not the real you, so stop internalizing it so much.

Using Your Imagination

Some of the most creative people of our time also have been the most anxious. These greats understood one important thing: **We can use our imaginations to help us, or to harm us**.

To the amygdala—that part of our brain responsible for the fight, flight or freeze response—everything is real, whether it's actually happening or just imagined. That's why it's important to not only change your thought patterns into new belief systems, but to learn empowering visualization skills (and combine imagination with deep breathing and proper posture).

Action Item: The imagination at work.

- Close your eyes and imagine yourself at your most confident, happy, and healthy best.

- Now notice the type of vibration you are emitting and stay with that feeling for 2 minutes.

- Whenever you use your imagination, your mind believes that what is happening is actually true, so the better you get at using your imagination in a positive way—and the more consistently you use this technique—the faster you'll turn from anxious to self-empowered.

CHAPTER 4

SELF-DIAGNOSIS AND THE DREADED MORNING FEELING

DON'T COMPLAIN ABOUT THINGS YOU'RE NOT WILLING TO CHANGE.

What a great time we live in, where any information is just a click away. The Internet is awesome! Or is it? For anxiety sufferers, the Internet can also be a dangerous addiction when used for self-diagnoses. In my case, as a hypochondriac and panic disorder sufferer, I was always looking online for a solution to my overwhelming panic attacks.

I could see something that read, "Have you checked your thyroid lately?" Then I'd start thinking, "Hmmm, thyroid? Not for at least six months... maybe THAT'S what's wrong with me!" Then I'd search the Internet for everything related to thyroid function–I'd join forums, send emails to doctors for feedback, and read every article I could find on the subject. I began to convince myself that I had a thyroid problem. Then I'd be back in the doctor's office again, this time for a thyroid test. After hearing that my thyroid was OK, I'd see a commercial on TV that mentioned strokes and the warning signs. What do you think I did next? Yep, went online, gathered all the information I could about strokes, and after a few hours, you guessed it, I had convinced myself I had all of the risk factors for a stroke, and back to the doctor I'd go. All of these doctor's visits came at the expense of inconveniencing my family, my boss, and my clients, but it didn't matter. I thought I had to be checked out immediately!

It's easy to see how the anxiety-produced habit of checking sensations, and researching them, can take over, but this course of action only leaves you feeling stranded and confused. There's a big difference between researching symptoms versus learning about your condition. In addition, there's the habit of sharing your story with other sufferers on the Internet, and looking to sites and chats each time a new facet of anxiety pops up. The problem with sharing your awful experiences, and how bad you're feeling, is that it doesn't help you feel any better, it just reinforces your current beliefs. Not only is it unhealthy for your thoughts and emotions, but eventually you will feel the physical effects as well. Just STOP talking to others about how bad you feel.

Researching Symptoms

At the onset of my anxiety disorder I was living in Milan, Italy, and was in a rut. The habit of over-worrying about my health, and researching symptoms online, was taking my focus away from tennis. This wasn't good because I had a coaching job teaching kids tennis 10 hours per week (in Italian) and the rest of my income came from tennis tournaments, so I had to stay focused during competition and the three hours of practice I put in each day.

At the lower levels of professional tennis, things like being in better shape than your opponent, having a better serve or forehand, or being a smarter player are only a small part of winning. What separates the winners from the losers are things like who eats better, sleeps better, doesn't get distracted, and has their equipment fully prepared before the match—those are the players who have a great advantage over the others. I had problems with all four of those components because I was overly concerned about my health.

If I didn't have an Internet connection during a tournament to check on my new symptoms, I simply wouldn't play that tournament, no matter how much money I could win and who my competition might be. Not surprisingly, this habit of overly worrying led to insomnia. Sleep disturbance is a key problem for roughly 55% to 75% of people with GAD and anxiety. The insomnia left me feeling mentally, physically and emotionally drained.

Insomnia

Thankfully, I was able to recognize the patterns that were keeping me awake at night and I applied methods to overcome it. In order for me to get a good night's sleep I had to train my mind to believe that the day was actually DONE once my head hit the pillow. The other piece of the puzzle was to stop putting so much pressure on myself about falling asleep.

I reminded myself that things didn't have to be perfect in order for me to get a good night's sleep. It was OK if I had had a panic attack, or didn't eat 100% clean—I still deserved a good night's rest. I started thinking about myself as a work in progress—I didn't have to try so hard to be perfect all the time, which removed a lot of pressure and helped me overcome the insomnia. This kind of reconditioning, though, didn't happen overnight.

A New Morning Routine

Morning was definitely the most challenging time of the day for me, as it is for many anxiety sufferers. The thought of facing another exhausting day was something I didn't look forward to. I felt sluggish, disappointed, and unmotivated. During my recovery phase, I remember waking up thinking that I should be feeling more joyful, less dizzy and more energetic, only to feel the same, if not worse, than I did the day before.

As difficult as this may sound, momentum in the morning is your best friend! I'm not suggesting you get up, sprint to the shower, gulp down your breakfast and rush out the door. What I am suggesting is that you DO NOT lie around all morning moping about how crummy you feel. It's time to change your morning routine.

In addition to your "Fresh Start" journal (to keep track of your negative thoughts), you need to physically have a fresh start to the morning. One of the new routines I did was to spend 5 minutes doing some kind of physical exercise, such as hip-twists, jumping jacks, sit-ups, push-ups, lunges, squats, running in place, riding a stationary bike, and bur-pees. This could be the most important 5 minutes of your day. Suck it up and make it a habit because it breaks your old state and negative mindset. Instead of waking up and playing the victim, you'll be taking charge and starting your day off on the right foot!

Exercise was one of my biggest challenges because all I felt like doing was sleep. Don't get me wrong, sleep is important in order to bring down anxiety levels, but adding in an exercise routine in the morning—as well as a few days a week in the afternoon or evening—takes you out of the victim role. You're stepping up and taking control.

After the new 5-minute routine, switch your morning around a little. Notice the usual way you do things and mix it up. If your current routine is breakfast, shower, tea, and then out the door, try exercise, shower, breakfast, tea, kiss the wife or husband, hug the kids, then off to work! Now doesn't that routine sound better? Mixing in a little exercise and some love will make a world of difference, but it must be done consistently.

There's one more thing that you need to change, and that's your bedroom, and I mean everything! If you're going to take back your life, you need to not be reminded of all of those mornings of suffering. When I walked into my bedroom with the bed in a different position, along with everything else, I had a feeling that things were changing for the better. I even bought a few paintings and quotes that I put up on the wall to remind me of how my life was changing for the better. This fresh change was also a good distraction from looking inwards and checking in. If you can't move everything around, just make small changes to the room, and have those changes be the strength that pulls you each morning to do your exercises and new morning routine.

In the end, these morning exercises and change of view in the bedroom will help loosen up your attitude. When you're so tightly wrapped up in trying to find an online cure or meeting people on forums who share the same anxiety levels as you, the Internet can definitely become a bad habit. You come to rely on it so much that that you forget what it's like to be free again; to take a spontaneous trip somewhere, to approach someone that you're attracted to, to learn a new language or even something as simple as going swimming.

After a while, you realize that you're being bluffed again and again by these thoughts and feelings that you believe are threatening you, when in fact it's all a lie. A big, fat lie! Take a look back at some of the times when you've suffered. Remember that time when you were out at a party and you started to feel a lump in your throat or dizziness and your mind began racing? At that moment your mind couldn't tell the difference between what was a real threat and what was imagined; it was just giving your body the signal to create more adrenaline in order to protect you and survive. Once you realize this, and stop running and fighting those anxious feelings, then you can start to let go and train your mind that what's happening is truly not life-threatening, and there's no need to react in that way anymore. That's the moment you start to take back your life, and the fake thing that you've created will shrink in size and become easily manageable.

Action Item: Create a new morning routine that calms your nervous system right away so your thought patterns begin to work in favour of rational thinking and optimism. Commit daily to a morning meditation session (there are plenty to choose from on The Anxiety Guy YouTube channel), a yoga session, or even a brisk walk while focusing on your deep breathing patterns. Repetition is key—the more you practice, the easier it will be to tap into your conscious mind throughout the day during more challenging events.

CHAPTER 5

IS IT REAL OR UNREAL? THAT IS THE QUESTION

**NINETY-NINE PERCENT OF ANXIETY RECOVERY
IS SEPARATING WHAT YOU DO FROM WHO YOU ARE.**

Have you ever felt like what you were doing, touching, or looking at, wasn't real? As previously mentioned, that's depersonalisation/derealisation, which is a recurring feeling of detachment from one's own body, as if in a dream. This is very common in people with anxiety disorders. For many years, it was my constant state, and at times it felt quite scary.

To get and idea of what it felt like to me like, imagine shaking your head side-to-side 20 times and not sleeping for 2 days straight. The result was that my thoughts slowed down, my response to a simple question was extremely challenging, and it was nearly impossible to explain how I was feeling to someone else who had never heard of depersonalisation/derealization. I wanted to rid myself of this nightmare so much so that I actually added more stress to the situation, which just perpetuated those awful experiences.

Eventually, I realised that my nervous system wasn't able to process all the stress I was putting myself under all at once, and the depersonalisation/derealization was my nervous system's way of forcing me to relax and slow things down. This was due, in the part, to my brain's amygdala, which is the main organ responsible for anxiety. Learning about depersonalisation/derealization helped me understand what was going on with me, but it still took some time until I was completely over this symptom.

Have a Laugh

Believe it or not, even the act of laughter from someone else can feel foreign to someone suffering from depersonalisation/derealisation. In fact, it's very common for sufferers to take action towards retraining themselves on how to laugh again; I had to. Laughter therapy comes in many creative forms and can have a huge impact on your recovery, but it's not only beneficial for people with an anxiety disorder. Anyone who wants to re-experience the childhood feeling of freedom, and bring looseness back into their lives, can retrain himself or herself to laugh again.

I remember going to a laughter-yoga class, and thinking, "How the heck does that work?" I found out that laughter yoga combines yogic breathing with unconditional laughter, and it started to transform me. The laughter in class was pure childlike playfulness, and it was contagious.

After 3 weeks of laughter-yoga class, I noticed that things started to become real again to me, and my unsteadiness was slowly subsiding—I was regaining my balance. The class was silly and I loved it. "Could laughter really be the best medicine?" I thought to myself. It certainly worked for me. So give yourself the gift of having a good laugh.

Action Item: Smiling, laughing, and happiness are skills.

- When was the last time you practiced strengthening the skills of smiling and laughing?

- If you suffer from anxiety, it's time to begin changing your emotional states, and the best way to start is by adding one small experience to your life that forces you to practice one of these positive states.

- What one thing are you willing to do every day this week? Go see a stand-up comic show? Sit on a bench and smile at the people walking by? Play with your kids, and practice happiness and staying in the moment? Watch a comedy? Take up a hobby you enjoyed as a child? Tell a few jokes to your friends or co-workers? Check out a laughter-yoga video online?

- Write down the actions you will commit to this week, and begin taking action to create a brand-new, exciting habit. It will help you feel more relaxed and less anxious.

CHAPTER 6

GET THE VAN READY!

**YOUR BIGGEST FEAR CONTAINS
YOUR GREATEST GROWTH.**

When it comes to professional tennis, most people think of the glamorous lives of the Top 50 players that they see on TV, but there are thousands of other professional-level players struggling at the bottom—fighting for each ATP tennis point they can get—hoping to play on the ATP circuit one day.

The futures tour mainly consists of players ranked between 500 and around 2000 on the ATP tour. Then comes the challenger-level players in the range of 150 to 500 roughly. If you can bear the years of struggle and grind, and are successful at the lower levels, then comes the ATP level.

My whole tennis career had mainly been in the futures level of tennis, with the very occasional "wild card" (a free pass for lower-level players to compete in higher-level tournaments) into a challenger event. I was able to play the pro events because I was successful in other prize-money events, which anyone could enter, and that provided just enough money for me to get from one tournament to the next…barely! But playing high-level tennis week after week left me emotionally, spiritually, mentally, and physically fatigued. I had to start taking care of the fatigue and reducing tension. Otherwise, I'd have a very short career in tennis.

Road Trip

At the age of 25, I got two of my friends together for a road trip in my rickety van. The plan was to play as many tennis tournaments as we could afford, and try to hang with other pro players. As we made the drive from Vancouver, British Columbia, to California, we decided to "wing it" and didn't book any housing. We only had $600 to cover all of our expenses (tournament entry fees, gas, food, and accommodations) for 45 days. It didn't take us long to figure out that we didn't have enough money.

We had put our faith into two "money" tournaments that we entered to get us through this trip in order to play four futures tennis tournaments. Many of the futures players don't stick around past their mid-20s; they get tired of the constant grind of the low-level tours. But we were different. We were determined!

The van was running well, and we had packed about a week's worth of food to get us by, but we needed a place to sleep. Since we were in California, we chose the beach: It was free, cozy, and warm. The next morning we rubbed off the sand, took a shower at the public restroom, and rushed off to find a tennis court. We were in Southern California, in the town of Ventura, about an hour north of Los Angeles. We found some courts, and lucky for us there was a hill right next to the courts, so we got some hard-core, uphill sprints in as well.

After practice, we saw a sign on the side of the road that said "29-cent tacos." Perfect timing! We ordered four tacos each. Once we were done eating, we were still hungry, so we ordered six more each. We were stuffed, and even though it was only noon, we decided not to spend any more money on food until the next day. We got back in the van and headed back to the beach, but this time we went north 30 minutes along the coast to the town of Santa Barbara.

As we rested on the beach, I started to feel sick. I blamed it on the tacos, but the other guys felt fine. I skipped afternoon practice in order to recover for our first tournament, which was the next day. That night, and as I closed my eyes to go to sleep, I used a technique that I did every time I had a match the next day—listening to a guided visualization.

Guided Visualization

If you suffer from anxiety, you're probably already using negative imagery, whether you're aware of it or not, but the opposite—positive imagery and visualization—is also available. Positive imagery is a great way to strengthen your inner resources during times of stress.

I think the most powerful method is to listen to a guided visualization, like I did on the beach that night. Because a lot of anxiety sufferers have a difficult time doing meditation or visualization on their own, due to over-sensitized nerves, I recommend using guided visualization during the first month of practice. That way the listener is directed by an experienced professional as to which images to bring to mind, and how to pace their breathing for perfect balance in mind and body. The idea is to take full control over your mind, rather than letting it control you.

Whenever I did a positive visualization the night before a match, it had an incredible effect on my performance the next day. With consistent visualization, you learn to be gentle and compassionate with yourself. After a great session, I was able to get the rest I needed in order to play well in the tennis match.

"Wake up," someone said. "WAKE UP!" It was the beach patrol, and they were not happy. I tried to explain our situation, but they told us that if they found us sleeping on the beach again, that we would be in big trouble. I didn't want to find out what kind of trouble that was, so we gathered up our stuff, threw everything in the van and headed to McDonald's for breakfast. After a $4 pancake-and-sausage breakfast, we went to the tennis site to check in before our matches. I was drawn up against a big-hitting collegiate player.

Me VS Myself

We split the first two sets and were headed into the third set. Because there had been a lot of line-call disputes during the game, we got a referee to sit and watch the final set so there wouldn't be any bad calls on crucial points. I had been extremely frustrated with my serve throughout the match, and I knew that if I had served just a little better this match would have been over, and in my favour, an hour ago. As the score reached 3 games to 1 for him, I hit my boiling point. After a missed serve by me, and a return by my opponent, I swung at the incoming ball with what felt like the hardest forehand I'd ever hit. It was cleanly struck and headed straight to where the chair umpire was sitting. It whizzed about 2 inches away from the referee's face; if it had hit him, I might have been in deep, deep trouble.

Then I heard the following words: "Disqualification, Mr. Simsek, for ball abuse." I didn't know what to say. I knew I'd had a moment of weakness, and my anger got the best of me. As I walked off the court, shaken by what I'd done, I promised myself I wouldn't let my anger take over my reactions again. What if I'd hit that poor guy? It would have haunted me forever.

My two friends also lost in their first rounds, so none of us won any prize money that day. As evening approached, we needed to find a place to stay. We had a few friends who lived in Southern California, but they didn't have enough room for all three of us.

Maybe we could find a hostel. We searched the Internet and ran into one in Santa Barbara not far from the beach and the public tennis courts. What a deal, we thought! A private room for the three of us was about $70 per night, although one of us had to sleep on the floor. We calculated how much money it would cost to stay at the hostel for the next week, and came to the conclusion that we had to make some extra money or we'd have to cut our trip short. Another week of training went by in Santa Barbara, and the next tournament was quickly approaching. It was in the city of Chico in Northern California.

Progressive Muscle Relaxation

The night before the match in Chico, I again did a guided visualization session, but this time I added progressive muscle relaxation (PMR). My junior tennis coach had told me about the benefits of PMR, so from time to time I used it when my muscles were stiffening up or I felt some tension in parts of my body.

The idea behind PMR is that by tightening, holding, and then releasing the major muscle groups in an exaggerated fashion, you end up feeling more relaxed and much less stressed and anxious. Consciously exaggerating and releasing muscle tension also helps you learn to recognize when you are holding on to unnecessary muscular tension so that you can use relaxation techniques to relieve stress before it gets out of hand.

If you have backaches, spasms, or significant injuries, first talk to a physiotherapist or your physician before starting a PMR session.

Action Item: Releasing Tension with PMR.

- Sit with your back straight and head in alignment with your spine.
- Plant your feet firmly on the floor and rest your hands on your lap.
- Beginning with your feet, tighten each muscle group for 15 to 20 seconds before completely letting go. Then pause 5 seconds before moving on to the next group of muscles.
- Work you way up from your feet to your ankles, knees, legs, and so on, until you get all the way up to your head. Then reverse the process, beginning with your head and going back down to your feet again.

I was placed in the qualifying round in the tournament in Chico. The first two rounds were a breeze. My third-round opponent was another collegiate player. I got off to a flying start and took the first set in 40 minutes. Since things were going in my favour, I started to relax too much, and my eyes wandered around the facility. Bad move. My opponent came back and won the second set 7-5. I eventually lost the match 6-4 in the third set.

After the match I found a tree and broke two of my three racquets out of frustration, much to the enjoyment of those watching. I was so angry with myself for letting my opponent back in the match, and missing the opportunity to get into the main event of the tournament.

That night our morale was low. My friends and I bought a case of beer, found a parking lot near the local university, and drank until we were numb. At that point, I had one racquet, $150 in my pocket, and some shoe goo to fix the holes in my tennis shoes. We got out of the van and walked towards the campus hoping to find a party that was free. We were in luck.

We met some college seniors headed to a house party, and decided to tag along. The party was fun, but in the back of my mind I was thinking about three things: How can we finish our trip without more money? Where can I find another racquet in case I break a string? And where are we going to stay? The last question was answered quickly. Apparently it's common for drunken students to pass out at a party house, so we found a spot, and went to sleep.

By the next morning, my buddies were getting home sick, and had lost the motivation to continue playing tournaments and roughing it. I couldn't blame them. They had enough money to catch a bus back to Canada, and later on that day they headed back home.

Now I was on my own. I reminded myself that one day I'd look back on this with great memories, no matter how difficult things were at the moment, so I continued. I asked each tournament director if it was OK for me to sleep in my van during tournaments, and I earned some money by stringing other players' racquets—it got me through to the end of my 6-week journey in California. Even though I didn't win any big victories or earn a lot of points, I felt like the trip was a success, because when things got tough, I persevered.

CHAPTER 7

I REFUSE TO LEAVE THIS HOUSE

YOUR PAST MISTAKES ARE MEANT
TO GUIDE YOU, NOT DEFINE YOU.

Thirty-one days! That's how long I spent at home one summer in my late 20s during the height of my anxiety and depression. I went outside in the backyard for fresh air, or a friend would come over for a barbecue, but other than that, I refused to leave the house.

In the movie "It's All Gone Pete Tong," the character Frankie Wilde is stuck at home trying to cure himself from going deaf. That's what I looked like after 31 days of being housebound. But, unlike Frankie, I was home for a different reason: I feared having a panic attack in public. I paid a deep price for this fear—financially, with my family and friends, and in my tennis career. I was so desperate for some sort of normalcy that I found some foam balls and made myself a little tennis court in the living room. I would play tennis against the wall to try and keep my timing up.

Living With Agoraphobia

The word "agoraphobia" is derived from the Greek words literally meaning "fear of the marketplace." It is an intense, irrational fear of being trapped in a situation where escape could be difficult or embarrassing; also it is a feeling of helplessness in the event of a panic attack. That certainly described me.

The fear of public places and wide-open areas makes a person suffering from severe agoraphobia live a life filled with avoidance of all kinds of potentially anxiety-causing situations, and may leave the victim homebound—as was my case. Agoraphobics quickly develop a feeling of hopelessness, and since agoraphobia is a manifestation of an anxiety disorder, it can lead to panic attacks. It's very common to feel symptoms such as light-headedness, rapid breathing, gastrointestinal distress (including nausea, vomiting, or diarrhea), rapid heartbeat, sweating, and chest pains when being trapped at home.

The National Alliance on Mental Illness reports that agoraphobia will affect approximately 5 to 12 percent of Americans at some point in their lives, and about 3.2 million Americans aged 18 to 54 are currently living with agoraphobia. Even famous people suffer from anxiety and agoraphobia. Kim Basinger once said, "When I came to Hollywood, I could wear a bikini, but I was in misery because people were looking at me. So I wore baggy clothes and watched other girls get the big parts and awards. I used to go home, play piano and scream at night to let out my frustrations. And this led to my agoraphobia."

Evolution of Agoraphobia

The agoraphobic associates a panic attack with the situation or place where it occurred, which leaves them trapped in their "comfort zone," which is their own home. Because of the possibility of another attack, a habit of non-trust in the outside world quickly develops. Unfortunately, the sufferer rarely talks about their fears, even to those closest to them.

Being agoraphobic, and having fear of places that might trigger panic attacks, was much, much scarier for me then my social anxiety. I was still able to communicate with people at a respectable rate, but others were constantly misunderstanding me. People started thinking I was a snob, or I was shy, and they treated me differently depending on the label they put on me. I wish I had had the guts to tell people how I really felt, but I was scared of being judged as crazy or weird, and I worried people might not want to have anything to do with me.

I later learned that people are much more caring and understanding then we think. Most people are incredibly caring, and just want what's best for you. So opening up about your fears and what's holding you back in life might be a good idea.

I was still stuck in my rut of being homebound for 31 days, and it wasn't until sometime later that I started to confront my fears and open up to people about what was going on. I was in my safe zone away from anything that would set off uncomfortable physical sensations of anxiety, but I knew in the back of my mind I had to start finding a way to take my life back.

Family History of Agoraphobia

I learned about agoraphobia in 1999 at the age of 19. My family had come from Turkey, and that year there was a massive earthquake that ripped through the city of Izmit, where my mom's family resided. It was a 7.6 magnitude quake that lasted 37 seconds. I knew that due to the condition of the buildings there, my family could be in trouble. The quake left half-a-million people homeless, and I was told that the tennis centre that I had trained at during our vacations to Turkey was completely underwater, along with many Turkish soldiers who I used to play tennis with. About 17,000 people died during the quake and 43,000 were injured.

We tried calling my grandparents and uncle, but there was no answer. A few days later, we finally got a hold of my grandma. She said the quake had happened while she was sitting on the patio of their house; suddenly she felt the apartment sway from side to side and heard the rumble of the apartment next door collapse to the ground, trapping and killing most of their friends and neighbours. My grandparents said their prayers and held each other as they huddled in their living room—they couldn't get out due to the swaying of the building. As they saw the other building next to them collapse, they held each other tighter, and accepted that their time was coming to an end.

My uncle was in another part of town and was outside during the quake. He later said that he felt like he was in a video game or movie as he watched the destruction all around him.

Then, an incredible thing happened. It stopped. They were alive.

Everyone in the apartment buildings next to my grandparents was killed. About 120,000 of these poorly engineered houses in Izmit were damaged beyond repair, another 50,000 houses were heavily damaged, and the other 2,000 buildings completely collapsed. The city was in shambles.

Soon after, my grandparents, aunt, and uncle found a shelter in the capital of Turkey and stayed there for a year. Eventually, my uncle couldn't stand the shelter anymore—there were so many people stuck there, so they all moved to Canada and stayed with us.

Once in Canada, my uncle saw a doctor and a few therapists, and was diagnosed with post traumatic stress disorder (PTSD). PTSD is a condition that can develop after a person has experienced or witnessed a traumatic event in which serious harm has occurred. People with PTSD often have persistent frightening thoughts and memories, and tend to feel emotionally numb, with a hazy view of the world.

War veterans were the first group to bring PTSD to the attention of the public, but PTSD can happen to anyone who witnesses or is involved in a traumatic event, such as an accident, a kidnapping, natural disaster, a mugging, violent attacks, rape, or losing a friend or loved one.

Depression is common in PTSD victims, and they can lose interest in things they once loved. Even day-to-day activities can make them feel edgy and distressed, due to sights, smells, or sounds that remind them of the event. These can trigger flashbacks and intrusive thoughts. Triggers can also be set off by certain feelings. Flashbacks occur in the form of nightmares, which can cause extreme anxiety and fear upon waking. PTSD sufferers often swing from feelings of intense emotion to no emotion at all, and this can greatly impact their relationships, friendships, and careers.

My uncle, for example, constantly woke up screaming in the middle of the night. He then became agoraphobic, and didn't leave the house for 3 weeks. To break the pattern, he gradually reintroduced himself to the outside world through **systematic desensitization**.

He started by going down the elevator to the bottom floor of our apartment. Then he took a step outside. Next, he went outside a little farther. Then, he walked to the end of the block and back. This progression continued until he overcame his fear of being outside in public again. It was amazing to witness. With that experience in the back of my mind, I was able to recognize agoraphobia in myself, and to know that there was hope for my own recovery.

Overcoming Agoraphobia

At the end of summer, my 31 days of agoraphobia came to an end. I had no choice; my time off from work was over. I knew it was time to face my fears. Here's what I did.

#1. I left my house, and forced myself to face the public places I feared most. Although I still avoided much of my friends and family in order to hide my condition, the overwhelming feelings of intense panic slowly subsided as I put effort into reconditioning a new mindset about the places I feared.

The first place I went to when I left my house was the grocery store. It seemed like killing two birds with one stone: overcoming my agoraphobia and being in a crowd, which normally was uncomfortable for me. As I walked the two long blocks to the store, I was aware of everything around me—from the cameras at the stoplights to the design on an old man's hat. I felt a little lost and confused, but then I thought, "Who cares! I've made a decision; I've learned from others who have overcome their struggles, and I'm ready to take on the world."

As I continued walking, I became more aware of my panicky sensations. My heart was pounding and dizziness kicked in, but this time I was prepared. I remembered the movie "The Gladiator," and how Maximus said, "Death smiles at us all. All a man can do is smile back." With that in my mind, and my immense fear of what the sensations might do to me, I smiled back. I had brought along a recording I made to remind me of three very important steps. First, simply allow the sensations to be present. Second, apply a challenge to a physical exercise—the physical exercise was power-walking to the store; the challenge was to get there in 7 minutes flat. And the final step was to let the storm pass.

I listened to the recording through my headphones over and over again while I reminded myself to stay focused on facing the fear and not running from it. I got to the grocery store, and accomplished my challenge of 7 minutes. I bought what I needed, checked out and then applied the same three steps on the way back. As I got home, I didn't care who was watching, I jumped around like a conquering hero! I welcomed the next challenges, rather than running from them, and I couldn't wait to feel that sense of accomplishment again.

#2. I created new meanings around what I was afraid of. Of course, it took time for my mind to accept the new data.

#3. I was proactive. I learned how to be a great problem solver, and not play the victim card.

#4. I focused on success stories. Tales about famous people who overcame anxiety provided a light at the end of the tunnel. For example, I learned that Abraham Lincoln was an extremely shy, self-doubting, and depressed individual for quite some time—just like I was!

Barbara Streisand had extreme social anxiety for 27 years, and reportedly spent more time in the recording studio then on stage due to fear. She gradually built up her confidence by singing in front of small audiences, and continued towards worldwide crowds in a short amount of time. Other famous people who have overcome their anxiety include David Beckham

(OCD), Oprah Winfrey (GAD), and Sigmund Freud (anxiety and hypochondria). I came to the conclusion that if they could do it, so could I.

#5. I surrounded myself with positive people. You don't overcome your fears by listening to people talk about what a victim they are, or how depressed their day has been. Sure, you can comfort them, but if you spend most of your time online, going from forum to forum, sharing your sob story with the world day after day, don't expect anything to change. I went to the people who had overcome their fears, and I followed how they did it. Inspiration is a powerful thing and it was the fuel for me when it came to ending my agoraphobia.

A great support team is absolutely vital. Expressing yourself consistently with someone who understands what it's like to have gone through a traumatic event—or a professional mentor/coach/therapist who has helped PTSD victims—will make the memories of the event less and less frightening. In the case of agoraphobia caused by PTSD, a treatment that works for one person, such as gradual desensitizing (as was the case with my uncle), may not work for another person. Some sufferers may need to try different treatments in order to find the one that works best for them.

When I'm playing a tennis match, I look for my opponent's weaknesses during the first 5 minutes of our warm up. Is he timing the shots better on his forehand than his backhand? Is he reacting negatively when he makes a mistake? This kind of information helps me develop my strategy. But what if he changes things up during the game? I look for his other weaknesses. In many ways, tennis is like a game of chess, and so is anxiety.

In my case, having dealt with agoraphobia for so long, I thought that if I stayed away from the things that I feared, and kept myself busy at home, then eventually my mind would forget about what I had been avoiding, and I would be free of agoraphobia once and for all. That was false.

Action Item: Avoidance of an environment, person, or situation only creates a deeper hole of fear and anxiety, and reinforces the idea that a true threat exists.

- Choose a situation that causes you some discomfort (shopping at a mall, meeting a friend for tea, going to a yoga class, etc.), and make a plan to do what you have been avoiding. By taking action, you begin to change the pairing in your mind of this activity or situation, from being a threat to being something neutral.

What I did, and what you must do too, is to step out of your comfort zone and meet your fears head on in small or large amounts (also called flooding in CBT). **Form a crystal-clear picture in your mind of how your life will be and how you will feel once you overcome your fears**, instead of thinking about how to continue arranging your life around your fears.

Everything we do is an attempt to feel more pleasure and less pain. Remember this; it's the feeling, not the thing that drives us.

CHAPTER 8

A LESSON IN FEAR

**COURAGE IS NOT THE ABSENCE OF FEAR.
IT IS ACTING IN SPITE OF IT.
—MARK TWAIN**

Do one thing every day that you fear. That was the challenge my dad gave to me near the end of my struggle with GAD. It's great advice when used properly, but people with anxiety disorders prefer to stay in their comfort zone. Unfortunately, staying in a bubble only leads to a limited life.

For example, if watching soap operas is an activity that doesn't lead towards being anxious or having a panic attack, the GAD person will continue to watch soap operas every day. If eating ice cream gives an anxious person temporary relief—even for a few minutes—he or she will eat ice cream every day.

These temporary retreats and unhealthy food can't give us what we're searching for deep down inside—a feeling of abundance in our lives. We all deserve to feel abundant every day in every way, yet our nervousness and temporary pleasures are preventing us from living life to the fullest.

Fear distorts our sense of what reality really is. It takes over our thoughts and drains us of our energy. The important thing to remember is that everyone experiences fear. The difference is that some people don't let fear control their lives, while others let fear control many aspects of how they live.

In people with panic and GAD, fear is a constant, but that fear rarely, if ever, manifests in reality. Anxious people give too much respect to a fearful thought, and therefore it grows in strength and eventually becomes chronic.

Action Item: Your thoughts are just thoughts, they are not reality.

- When you have a thought that is negative, pessimistic, or irrational, start to create doubt around that thought. Choose a thought that's controlling your emotional state right now, and start to consistently create doubt around it by asking yourself questions about its validity. Replace the negative thought by building evidence of a new, more-empowering thought.

- Example of an irrational thought: I'll never be liked by anyone!

- The doubt-provoking replacement: I have many friends, and shouldn't generalize based around just one experience.

In the beginning, I didn't leave my house because of the fear of having a panic attack and embarrassing myself. I didn't get on a plane for fear of it crashing. In a building, I didn't go higher than the 10th floor because of my fear of heights. And I wouldn't visit a city that could potentially be hit with an earthquake. To say I feared life is an understatement. I went through my daily routines in my comfort zone and didn't dare change them, unless I had no other choice. Life was meaningless and boring, until I heard about an Englishman named Richard Branson.

Sir Richard Branson is well known for being a successful entrepreneur and the founder of the Virgin Group. He is also a man who is known to be fearless. After I saw a documentary about how Branson set off around the world in a hot-air balloon race, I was hooked. How come he wasn't lying around on a beach somewhere enjoying his fortune? Was this guy nuts? Why was he risking his life doing all of these mind-blowing stunts?

I highly recommend his book, "Screw It, Let's Do It." I've read it a few times, and it brought a lot of motivation to my life—it could do the same for you. I learned that if we let things terrify us, life isn't worth living. So, I made the decision to conquer my fears one by one.

30-Day Anxiety Challenge

I made up my mind that for the next 30 days I'd do one thing I was terrified of every day. In order to keep myself motivated, I established a punishment system: If I didn't conquer a fear that day, I could only have veggie shakes the next day (I didn't like veggie shakes back then).

I created a list of all the things that I feared—like approaching 5 strangers and starting a conversation that would lead to a meet-up elsewhere (to help with my social anxiety); having a group of members at my tennis club taunt and laugh at me while playing (to get over my fear of being judged and embarrassment); giving a seminar to 50 people on the topic of anxiety (fear of public speaking); and holding a spider in my hand for a minute (I hate spiders more than anything!).

The challenge started working for me. The feeling I had after conquering a long-held fear was indescribable. I was building up momentum and confidence, which opened up more and more doors for me in terms of new life experiences.

If you decide to take on your own 30-day Anxiety Challenge, you will begin to look at the fearful and negative thoughts that have run your life in a different way. It's important that you do the challenge the right way, though. There should always be a set amount of time put on each challenge that will push you towards your emotional limit.

One of the biggest challenges I made for myself had to do with what I feared most—bodily sensations during a panic attack. Just the thought of how real they felt, and how hopeless I felt during the build-up and peak of a panic attack, was too much for me to handle. Or was it?

Sensations are not dangerous, and a panic attack is a sign of a healthy and reactive body.

First, I had to think of a place that caused me great anxiety—a place where I had terrible panic attacks that eventually sent me the ER. The shopping mall was perfect for this challenge.

Second, I needed to draw out a fearful symptom. I always had a slight headache, felt dizzy and had heart palpitations, so those weren't sensations that drove me to the nearest exit. It was the feeling of choking and being short of breath that bothered me the most.

I found a spot at the mall to sit down and draw that feeling towards me. I focused my attention on a spot across from me and waited. About 20 minutes later, what I feared most hit its peak and came screaming towards me. As much as I wanted to run, I sat there for a few moments and then rushed out looking for help.

I headed home, shaking and sweating uncontrollably, and spent the rest of the day in bed. Remembering how much I dreaded crowded areas and wasn't good at sitting still, I decided that I had done fairly well in facing my biggest fear.

Action Item: A mindfulness exercise to lessen the anxiety response.

- Sit in a quiet, comfortable spot where you won't be disturbed. Take 3 deep, slow breaths (eyes open is fine).

- As you settle into a natural breathing rhythm, allow any sounds you hear to just pass through your awareness.

- Relax your attitude and let go of any expectations or judgments of this practice.

- Notice how your mind wanders, and jumps from thought to thought.

- Gently bring your attention back to your stomach or chest, and feel them rise as you breath in. Breathing out, feel them fall.

- Continue this practice, observing the sensation of the in- and out-breath.

- When the mind wanders, again release the thought, and return your focus to your breath.

- Become comfortable with the stillness; just sitting and breathing.

- After 5 to 7 minutes, take 3 deep breaths and slowly begin to move.

Jimmy Carter once said, "It's not necessary to fear the prospect of failure, but to be determined not to fail." Determined I was, because I accomplished my fear of choking in a crowded place challenge after a dozen more tries. The amount of time I had set for that challenge was 15 minutes without movement. It was a huge turning point on my path to recovery. Finally, I accomplished my 30-day challenge. It actually took me 45 days, but I was ecstatic.

I felt like a cat with 9 lives (more like 40 lives the way things had been going). As I went through my 30-day challenge, I slowly felt the walls of worry, fear, and anxiety start to crumble away slowly as my confidence started to rise.

Flooding

I'm sure you've heard "experts" warn anxiety sufferers to stay away from caffeine. Well that was the next challenge on my list: one large cup of black coffee in the morning, and one cup in the evening. My fiancée, Robyn, thought I was nuts, and packed a bag for the ER that night, which is where I usually landed after consuming caffeine. It made me extremely jittery and mirrored an oncoming panic attack better than anything else. This led to thoughts like, "Oh no! There's that awful feeling again," and "What's that tingling in my arm?" And then I'd feel a huge lump in my throat as well as shortness of breath.

That night, after my coffee challenge, I slept like a baby. The reason was that I finally recognized a connection to my panic and anxiety. Unlike in the past—when my thoughts and fears bluffed me and I gave into them thinking that I was in life-threatening danger—this time I remembered that what I was feeling was simply due to the caffeine in the coffee.

I went on to use that connection in different situations. For example, if I were speaking to someone, who in the past made me feel anxious and uncomfortable, instead of it leading to a panic attack, the coffee challenge popped into my head, and I knew that those thoughts and physical feelings were just false alarms that needed to be ignored and replaced with realistic, positive thoughts. This always sent my physical sensations away; or, at least, I didn't pay attention to them if they were there.

Systematic Desensitization

In my 30-day challenge, I dove headfirst into my fears. That's because I didn't know at the time about a step-by-step, gradual system called "systematic desensitization." If I had known about it, I definitely would have taken this less-frightful path.

Systematic desensitization assumes that fears and phobias are learned, and that they can be unlearned through controlled exposure to the fear or phobia. The process slowly takes away the person's sensitivity to the feared object. Systematic desensitization starts with clearly recognizing what the fear is, and then making a ladder in the form of a hierarchy—from least scary to the ultimate goal—with 10 action steps for each fear.

In the case of claustrophobia and a fear of elevators the ladder might look like this:

1. Picture an elevator in your mind.
2. Look at a silly drawing of someone in an elevator.
3. Look at a real, more-serious drawing of someone in an elevator.

4. Look at a real photo of someone in an elevator.
5. Find and look at a real elevator up close.
6. Take a step into an elevator and then step back out.
7. Go up one floor (with a friend to accompany you) in an elevator.
8. Go up to the top floor (with a friend to accompany you) in an elevator.
9. Go up one floor on your own in an elevator.
10. Finally, go up to the top floor by yourself in an elevator.

As you can see, the person begins with the step that causes only small amounts of very manageable anxiety, and from there slowly exposes him or herself to more and more challenging scenarios.

I've always been big on tattoos, and had a few from over the years. One day, after a yoga session, I read a quote on the wall that said, "All power is from within and is therefore under our control." I thought it was a perfect quote for dealing with fear, so I had it tattooed on my forearm. It served as a reminder that all the tools I needed to change my past nightmares were within me.

Once I tapped into that power with the momentum I gained from the tools that I used in my new daily life, I was eventually able to completely let go of panic and GAD. Of course it wasn't a straight road to freedom from anxiety. My mind and body put up a huge fight; determined to suck me back into the old worry and fear cycle of bodily sensations. This quote was just another form of strength that I pulled from when my past popped up. I'm not suggesting you get a tattoo, but I am suggesting that you to surround yourself with things that keep you on the right track.

CHAPTER 9

THE PROS AND CONS OF BEING AN ATHLETE

YOU DON'T HAVE TO BE CONFIDENT—YOU HAVE TO BE RELENTLESS AND DETERMINED.

The mental, physical, and emotional benefits of being an athlete are endless. But those benefits aren't just for athletics. What have you committed to that you're proud of? What lessons did it teach you? How can you apply that to your Natural Anxiety Recovery? Take a look at the list that follows and consider how you can begin working on these elements as you move towards control over your thoughts, words, emotions, and behaviours.

Physical Benefits

Body Image—Research done through the President's Council on Physical Fitness and Sports shows that kids involved in sports are more likely to have a positive image of their body and higher self-esteem. It also plays a big part in keeping the child from being overweight. Of course, the same goes for adults.

Overall Health—Children who engage in sports tend to continue physical activity later on in life. Cardiovascular disease, diabetes, cancer, hypertension, obesity, depression, and osteoporosis can be curbed with the help of regular physical activity. The benefits are, of course, endless in many forms.

Mental & Emotional Benefits

Self-discipline—That's something nobody can really teach you; it's something that you gain by following your passion and having a clear image in your mind of what you want the outcome to be, and then taking action in a way that isn't self-destructive. It teaches you the importance of preparation, and that life can be unpredictable. Most importantly, it teaches you that it's OK to fail, and that greatness in any sport, or occupation, is measured by how a person reacts to failure. Then, the pressure to be perfect is lifted.

Problem Solving—Athletes learn to be proactive and see problems before they arise. They also get good at problem solving. By the time I was 18, I was able to become my own coach on and off the court. Just like you are learning to become your own CBT or NLP practitioner or counsellor in your life. I am grateful for the benefits I received from being an athlete, but there were the inevitable challenges

Physical Challenges

Injuries—During my teens, if I didn't wake up with an ache or soreness of some type, I knew I hadn't worked hard enough the day before. Athletes don't have time for injuries or excuses. They learn that success is measured by getting up one more time after you feel like you can't (similar to the anxiety battle in your mind between fear and faith). Playing through injury built up toughness in me that I was able to use when I felt emotionally and mentally injured during my anxiety disorder days.

Exhaustion—This means you have pushed your mind and body to a point where you simply can't push any further. Exhaustion is generally present during anxiety disorders, and willpower can be a very limited resource.

Athletes understand that pain is temporary, and exhaustion is part of the process of reaching a goal. Non-athletes don't typically do so well; when exhaustion strikes after a long workday, for example, many people get caught in the cycle of playing the victim. But you can adopt the mindset of the mental greats by doing the following: find a proven method based around CBT or NLP, make the decision to change, commit to the method, end the excuses, and fall in love with progress. From there, you'll come to see each blip along the road as a sign that you're moving in the right direction.

Mental & Emotional Challenges

Criticism—Athletes are always faced with criticism. My first tennis coaches told me I'd never be a professional player because I was too small, and my fellow tennis players said I was too skinny. When I got older, I was afraid of criticism because it added to my high levels of anxiety. But the fact is that we're all going to be judged by others, no matter what.

Overzealous Trainers/Coaches—Many coaches put too much emphasis on making kids into technical wizards, and the young athlete quickly loses interest because the fun is sidelined.

High Expectations/Pressure–Some kids thrive under the pressure to perform as a young athlete, but most just want to hide somewhere. When high expectations are placed on results, the young athlete over-focuses on the end result instead of the process of developing as a person. The feeling of letting parents, friends, coaches, or trainers down by losing can weigh heavily on the shoulders of an athlete.

Weighing the Pros and Cons

An athlete who grows up with a support group (parents, coaches, other players, etc.) that prioritizes long-term success, enjoyment, connections, teamwork, and persistence over short-term expectations, all-or-nothing thinking, instant results, and individualism, is much more likely to become a well-balanced individual and a great athlete. Even with a dedicated support group, it still takes four very important steps in order to become a successful athlete and human being: it's the three P's.

Perfect Practice—Forget the old the saying, "practice makes perfect" and replace it with "perfect practice makes perfect." The quality of your practice (and the implementation of your skill sets for overcoming anxiety) is what separates good athletes from great athletes. Andre Agassi, the former #1 tennis player, said that in his prime, he only practiced on the court 45 minutes a day. Imagine what kind of quality was in those 45 minutes.

Persistence–Sports teach people many great life lessons, but none more than persistence. Singer/actor Will Smith said, "The only thing that I see that is distinctly different about me is I'm not afraid to die on a treadmill. I will not be out-worked, period. You might have more talent than me, you might be smarter than me, you might be sexier than me, you might be all of those things you got it on me in nine categories. But if we get on the treadmill together, there are two things: You're getting off first, or I'm going to die. It's really that simple, right?"

Now that's persistence. It's being clear about your goal and relentlessly chasing it no matter what. Apply persistence to your anxiety recovery, fall in love with your daily progress, and you'll begin to gain the belief within you that you never thought was possible.

Patience—"Patience and time do more than strength or passion," Jean de La Fontaine once said. Patience is a quality that many people struggle with—whether or not they have an anxiety disorder. They growl and huff and puff every time a car in front of them doesn't move fast enough when a traffic light turns green. Needless to say, patience does not come easily to most of us due to the fast paced world we live in and the demands that are placed upon us from many different angles, it's probably harder now to be patient than historically it has ever been. As an athlete patience can be a huge challenge but this is where a great team of supporters comes in to keep you looking farther ahead.

One of my greatest idols I looked up to growing up was basketball legend Michael Jordan. He said, "Some people want it to happen, some wish it would happen, others make it happen."

Action Item: Understand the 3 P's, and recognize which one needs a deeper amount of focus from you on a daily basis:

- Perfect Practice
- Persistence
- Patience

Once you recognize which one you're lacking, create awareness throughout the day of the best times to implement the practice of Perfect Practice, Persistence, and Patience.

CHAPTER 10

WHAT I LEARNED FROM ANDRE AGASSI

DON'T LET YOUR STRUGGLE BECOME YOUR IDENTITY.

Andre Agassi turned pro at the age of 16. He was the only male player in history to win all four of the grand slams of tennis and an Olympic gold medal. He was also inducted into the International Tennis Hall of Fame. But Andre was much more than a tennis player to me.

I grew up watching every match I could that Andre played in. I saw him on the tennis court with his long flowing hair, and immediately asked my mom how I could grow my hair quicker (coconut oil, thanks mom!). He wore flashy neon spandex shorts and shirts that screamed oil spill. I begged my parents to buy outfits like Andre's, but they were too expensive, so I had to make my own. I'd find an old towel, cut it up to make a headband, and draw the same designs as Andre had on his. The other players made fun of me, but I didn't care; I felt like a tennis rock star!

While I was with the Canadian national junior team in Europe, I watched a match on TV that Andre was playing in. I was a few hours from walking on the court to compete in a tournament. Technique is something in tennis that takes years to master, and proper repetition in practice is key. Try telling that to a kid who wants to be like his idol on the court. After watching Andre's match, I found a backboard to warm up, but I didn't use my regular strokes; I tried to emulate Andre's forehand, backhand, serve, and his between-the-leg shot.

I only had 30 minutes until a very important match, and I had completely changed the way I played, but it felt so good! I took to the court as my coach sat courtside. Andre's famous line was "image is everything," so I decided to focus on my image and replicate Andre's shots, his quick pigeon-toed walk, his mannerisms, everything, and forget about the end result of that match—now that's love.

Not surprisingly, my opponent crushed me. After the match, my coach said, "What the hell was that, Andre?" I stood there, with my head down, and after a few deep breaths I looked up at him and asked, "Did I really look like Andre?" Needless to say, our player/coach relationship was iffy after that.

Andre and I had similar upbringings: our dads both started us in the game. He started playing at the same age I did, and we both grew up with similar daily routines—tennis before school, tennis during school, tennis after school, watch tennis, brush your teeth, go to bed. He portrayed the rebel and wasn't always liked by everyone because of his outrageous attitude and outfits, but he didn't seem to care about what others thought. He did what he wanted, and so did I. I always hoped to watch him live, and I was about to get my opportunity.

My chance to see Andre live came true during a pro tournament in Toronto. That wasn't the only great news, though—the coordinators of the event had a relationship with my dad, and I was going to be one of the ball kids for Andre's match! I nearly fainted. Holy smokes!

After a few days of rigorous ball-kid training I was ready. Andre had a night match, and I was extremely nervous. My parents tried to calm me down, but there was no point—it was like meeting a tennis god.

The stadium court was ready, and Andre was minutes away from walking down the stairs to the court. I was practicing some last-minute ball-boy exercises, anxiously waiting for him, and then it happened. Escorted by a security team, Andre appeared at the top of the steps and a huge roar went off from the crowd. I couldn't believe it. My eyes were glued to his every step down the stairs. As he got to the bottom, he waved to the crowd and we all took our positions. There he was, just a few metres away from me. I could feel my heart pounding and sweat racing down my forehead. It was my dream come true.

As Andre started his warm-up, I was slightly behind and to the right of him, but I wasn't paying attention to the balls flying by, because I was so focused on him. I was also his towel boy on one side of the court, so anytime he needed to towel-off I'd run and give him his towel and then run back.

The first few games went smoothly. It felt incredible being on the court witnessing how hard the tennis ball went after it impacted Andre's racquet strings.

Of course I had a few blips during the match. One time I ran to pick up a ball near Andre's feet and I tripped and almost fell over, but I held my balance and kept going. The crowd got a chuckle out of that one. As the match ended, and Andre walked over to his bench, victorious, I had an overwhelming urge to ask him for his racquet. I mean, what was the worst that could happen? He'd say no? Actually, that would have been kind of devastating, but who could say no to a kid, right? Plus, it would be one of the bravest moments of my life. Just as I was about to pop the question, a crew of interviewers swarmed him and I lost my chance. After the interview, Andre quickly left the grounds.

Heading home after that match, I had an incredible feeling of gratitude—I realised dreams really can come true. It was a life-changing night that I'll never forget.

Through Andre's rebellious years on the pro tennis circuit, winning Grand Slam after Grand Slam, he admitted to hating the game of tennis. When I heard this, I was shocked and sad. How could he be so successful and not enjoy himself on the court? More specifically, Andre was at a crossroads in his life at the peak of his human athletic ability. His ranking was dropping outside of the Top 100, and he hadn't won a Grand Slam championship for over 2 years. Andre could have easily quit the sport at that point, but he didn't. He used tennis as a vehicle to further understand who he was as a person and started to make a comeback.

Andre wasn't born a champion; he had to work hard to become a champion. He never had the quickest foot speed, or the biggest serve, but he made up for those with his strengths, which were the ability to "see" the ball better than anyone else in the world, and the ability to rush his opponents by taking the ball earlier than anyone else, and forcing them into submission slowly as the match went on. It was truly incredible to watch.

For Andre, growth was more important than success, and that was the reason he came back and rose to the top of the sport again after his darkest days—because of self-growth.

His life made me think about my own struggles. I never made it to the levels in tennis that Andre was playing, not by a long shot, and I started to question the reason why I was trying to play professional tennis through my 6-year struggle with anxiety, and get my ATP point once and for all. Was I trying to please others? No. Was it because this sport was my identity, and if I quit, then maybe people wouldn't take me seriously anymore? That wasn't it, either. The reason I kept at it was because people said I couldn't do it—that's why.

My fellow players and coaches kept telling me how the game had changed, and how I was getting too old to compete. They said I needed to stop "living the dream." But my decision was clear—I couldn't live with the idea of regretting this the rest of my life if I stopped competing, and, like Andre, I learned a lot about myself throughout those tough years.

Off the court, Andre taught me how important it is to help others. In 1994, he created a school for disadvantaged teens in his hometown of Las Vegas, Nevada, named the Andre Agassi Foundation. It's an organization that focuses on transforming public education for the underserved youth in Las

Vegas. In addition to that, Andre did much more for others throughout his life. He taught me that even the smallest acts of kindness make a difference in other people's lives. We can get so caught up in building our career, or chasing certain things that we forget that the most important reason why we're here is to give back.

Action Item: One of the 6 human needs is contribution. Think of how you can contribute to helping others in some way, and pick a day within the next few weeks to take action. Some examples include: volunteering at a children's hospital, helping a friend who's struggling with an area of their life, or creating a meet-up for people to network for free.

Service Decreases Anxiety

Giving back and helping others greatly helped me overcome my anxiety disorder. When I taught junior tennis players, there were times when I'd have to travel long distances with my students, and I paid for those trips out of my own pocket because I knew how valuable it was to the kids for me to attend those events. Helping others, whether it's kids or adults, is a great opportunity for anxious people to turn their focus away from their internal worries. As Anthony Robbins says, "Where focus goes, energy flows." When the focus is put towards helping and inspiring others, a huge weight is lifted from your shoulders and a feeling of accomplishment and gratitude takes its place.

Action Item: Is your focus currently more on your internal world, or your external world? What types of results are you getting? If you're stuck in thoughts, sensations, or future events, you're very internal, which means it's time to turn your attention to things happening externally around you. If you're very external, and your emotional mind is running the show through anger and anxiety over things happening in the external world, you'll have to begin turning your attention towards your internal world to gain more self-control in those moments. Create some self-awareness; write down where your focus has been going, and change the habit if it needs to be changed.

CHAPTER 11

A SUBCONSCIOUS CHANGE OF VIEW

**YOU HAVE ALL THE RESOURCES WITHIN
YOU TO CREATE THE CHANGE YOU DESIRE.**

Is it possible for two people to look at the same thing and have different opinions? Yes, and each person's point of view will potentially determine what their future experiences will be. Can we also apply this to GAD? Definitely. Are you looking at life the wrong way?

No Man's Land

In tennis, there's an area of the court called "no man's land," and it's the worst place to return the ball. However, new players don't know this, and tend to stand there. Instead of hitting at the net, or at the baseline like the pros, they stand right where their opponent can hammer the ball at their feet. Once they learn the right places to stand, they can return hits.

Likewise, there is a similar place in life called "no man's land," where it's easier not to feel anything. In my experience, working with people to overcome their GAD and panic, I've found that anxiety sufferers have the least amount of emotions due to the fear of feelings. They do this purposely. The fear of more loss, or disappointment, keeps anxiety sufferers in an emotional "no man's land." Basically, they think that if they stay in that "middle area" where they don't feel too happy or too sad, then they won't feel disappointed in the end. Of the few emotions these people do feel, most are negative.

People who don't suffer from anxiety are more willing to explore the highs and lows of daily emotions. They also know how to bring themselves out of a negative state quickly, whereas a GAD sufferer has a much more difficult time getting out of a negative funk.

Gradual Negative Build

During the ages of 26 to 31, I was consumed by negativity. My view of the world was all bad, but it didn't happen overnight. There was a gradually build up from listening to and believing the internal chatter inside my head. I generalized people very quickly, and I believed no one cared whether I lived or died. What an awful way to go through life! During those years, I got more of what I complained about, more of what I feared, and more experiences with negative people. I was playing the same record over and over again, day after day.

From Negative to Positive

Changing the way you see something to bring about a more positive view can have an amazing snowball effect, and it's not uncommon to see the positive difference in other aspects of life, without even thinking about it.

I threw a tennis event for some people who I was working with to help get over their GAD and panic disorder. It brought in a few hundred people, and some of them were doing better than others in their recovery. I wanted to know the main reasons why some were succeeding faster than the others. I got into a 20-minute conversation with 6 of them to find out.

Three were still struggling to take their first steps (and were still experiencing full-blown panic attacks almost daily), and the others were completely different people compared to who they once were. Keep in mind that they all started off at a level of 8.5 to 10 on the anxiety scale just a few months earlier. I didn't ask them anything about their anxiety, their fears, or sensations. What I did discover was that the group that wasn't progressing as fast kept bringing up how bad their anxiety was, whereas the successful group was directing the conversation to anything in their outer world that had little to do with themselves.

I also tested their view on something both sides had struggled with—the fear of any feeling related to the heart. All of their original complaints were very similar: a pounding heart, almost like a continuous heart palpitation. They were so aware of their beating heart that they'd hold their pulse, do breathing exercises, pray, do anything so that they wouldn't experience that feeling.

When I asked the question, "Has a fear of a heart attack crept in at all lately?" I heard two very different answers. Someone in the group that was farther ahead in their recovery said, "I questioned whether a hard heart beat was scarier than a soft heartbeat. A soft heartbeat would make me feel like I was dying, and wouldn't give me the feeling that my most important muscle, my heart, was very strong. A hard heartbeat now gives me assurance that I'm in good shape, and that I can feel good about the strength of my heart muscle. Instead of fearing my hard heartbeat, I now look for it, and recognize that like any muscle, it needs to be exercised to stay strong." What an incredible change of view!

Something so simple as changing the meaning of something can almost instantly turn our whole world around, and bring to us the experiences in life we crave. Someone from the other group had this response, "Yes, my fear is still there, and every time I get a feeling in my heart, I get scared and think the worst. I haven't yet accepted that this pounding is caused by anxiety. Since I'm now a runner, I feel the same pounding heart during my runs but it doesn't seem to affect me during my runs."

Conscious vs Subconscious

I found out something else from these two groups. One group was putting more effort into trying to change their views of the world not only consciously, but subconsciously as well.

If you are constantly worried about something—like your health—your conscious mind continually focuses on your **lack** of health. It attaches an emotion to it—in this case fear—and is stored in the subconscious mind as reality. This belief then sends a vibratory output related to lack, and begins to attract life events and circumstances based around that belief. Therefore, reconditioning your subconscious mind can rewire the programs that are currently running your physical world.

If you don't tap into the power of your subconscious, then you're missing out on a huge part of recovery from anxiety; maybe one of the biggest.

Thomas Edison said, "Never go to sleep without a request to your subconscious."

We are continually planting seeds (thoughts) in our subconscious based on our habits of thinking. When my conscious mind was full of fear and anxiety, my subconscious mind flooded me with panic and hopelessness, which created a cycle that overtook me.

I asked the successful group, "What did you find was the best way to change the meaning, and your view, of a pounding heart?" "Auto suggestion with authority," one of the participants said. She explained that she read statements out loud of what she desired most, and her new view about her pounding heart. In order for this to take hold in her mind, she did it several times each day with incredible emotion and focus. By reading to herself aloud with authority, she built enough power behind it to really create change.

Here are two more examples of people who started with similar debilitating anxiety levels.

One person trained a new perspective that eventually took all the fear of a pounding heart away. This man was able to see that a calm heart would actually be much scarier than a pounding heart. Now, when he doesn't feel his heart pounding, he wonders why, and immediately does something physical, such as running or biking, to strengthen his heart muscle so he can actually feel that pounding sensation. He's been able to go of this feeling because he replaced his greatest worrying sensation with something that could be more fearful, and he trained his subconscious mind. This required repetition to create change.

The other example, a woman who ran daily, wasn't able to desensitise herself from her pounding heart because she didn't apply the knowledge of why her body reacted with a pounding heart, nor did she adopt a different perspective in order to train her subconscious.

Auto Suggestion

More and more athletes are utilizing the benefits of tapping into their subconscious mind. Look at Ray Lewis, an all-star line backer in football. He repeatedly uses autosuggestion to ramp up himself and his teammates before each game so that they get into a peak state. It's not just once in a while—he does it during the intros, the warm up, during the game, and after the game. He has programmed himself and his teammates to become fearless.

What about Muhammad Ali? He created fear in his opponents and had an amazing record—not because he was the hardest puncher, but because he continuously fed his subconscious mind with autosuggestions that were scary!

The path to my full recovery from anxiety is best described by one of Ali's great quotes: **"It isn't the mountains ahead to climb that wear you out; it's the pebble in your shoe**." The pebble in my shoe was fear, so take this book and apply it to your life so that you reach the top of the mountain.

CHAPTER 12

DIET & DETERMINATION

**WHAT CONSUMES YOUR MIND,
CONTROLS YOUR LIFE.**

A hypochondriac never believes a doctor's clean-bill-of-health report, and I was no exception. I fiercely held my ground, letting each and every healthcare provider know that I really was physically sick, and all the tests were wrong. It was a battle, and at that time I should have paid closer attention to building on those facts—that there was nothing to fear, and it was "all in my head," as many had told me.

But back then my thoughts could easily and quickly overtake me. I felt powerless to stop them. Some of the thoughts were, "Remember a few days ago, when you started feeling sensations?" and "What if you start experiencing shortness of breath and tingling feelings in your arms? Could it be a heart attack this time?" Finally the most common one of all, "Where can I run to in case of a panic attack?" Then things would begin to spiral out of control.

Me VS Myself

It's difficult for someone with GAD to explain why he or she needs to leave a situation; so I'd come up with a lie, such as, "I have to go ASAP because Robyn needs my help at home and she isn't feeling well." During a warm up at a tennis match in Vancouver, I knew there would be a large crowd and that it would also be on TV. I was in full-on panic; experiencing such extreme dizziness that each tennis ball that came towards me looked like it had multiplied in to multiple balls. I could barely hang on to my racquet, let alone the situation.

I decided to pull myself together somewhat, tell a lie (that I had a bad shoulder injury that wouldn't allow me to play), and send home hundreds of excited people who came to watch. Goodbye potential trophy, goodbye tennis ranking, and goodbye pride.

There I was, yet again, making up lies to deal with panic. I knew I had to get help. I drove a few blocks before pulling the car over and getting on my hands and knees to try to catch my breath, and fight the tingling feeling in my arms and chest, as well as the awful dizziness. I called 911. Within minutes an ambulance arrived and started attending to me.

"What's wrong?" they asked. I listed it all off one by one. The emergency workers had an idea of what was going on, and brushed aside a number of my complaints. "Do you want us to drive you to the hospital or would you like to drive yourself?"

"Drive myself? Are you mad!!!" I hopped in the ambulance and off we went to the nearest hospital. Then came the usual procedure of checking my blood pressure and my breathing, followed by a battery of tests that included things like a stress test, ECG, blood tests, a chest X-ray, throat ultrasound, and heart ultrasound, just to name a few. As I lay there with needles and wires in my body, I wondered, "How did I get to this point? I should be at work helping and mentoring kids through a wonderful sport, loving the fact I get to stay in shape and be active in my career, and then look forward to going home and spending a wonderful evening with my family."

Unfortunately, that was the dream and it was far from my reality. After 6 hours of being in the ER waiting and doing tests, I was told there was nothing more they could do. All the tests came back negative and I was free to go home. I felt a massive amount of relief. I felt happy, calm and relieved, and my panic subsided, but what if they missed something?

I was no stranger to the ER. From the ages of 26 to 31, I had logged over 50 visits; sometimes before and after tennis matches. The ER visits were due to either a bad panic attack caused by a situation from the past that triggered panic, or a scary physical sensation. I didn't pick up on the chain of thoughts and why the cycle kept going day after day. The way I interpreted the world around me, and the judgments I made of things, was being stored in my subconscious. I played the same recording over and over, day after day without a break, and ultimately paid the price through these panic attacks and GAD.

My emotions, as they were happening, **were just signals** that I needed to react to the current situation. If I was feeling scared, for example, I should have looked at the root cause of that emotion, not the situation I was in at that moment.

All main emotions have secondary emotions that are usually causing them. I should have tried to understand what secondary emotions might be coming into play during any of the times when I felt upset or anxious. We don't feel emotions "for no reason." There is usually a trigger that sets off a secondary emotion, which then builds up with all of the other feelings that have been suppressed, and this causes an emotional reaction that seems out of sync with what is currently being experienced. The key here is to be aware of those deep-seated, underlying secondary emotions that are causing negative feelings, and deal with those first.

Once you pay attention to those feelings, you can turn them around and begin to improve your overall outlook. Knowing what causes your negative feelings can move you towards ending the cycle of GAD and panic attacks.

More Doctor's Visits

I began not mentioning my anxiety to doctors, just so they wouldn't order the same tests again and again. I thought that if they gave me a different test, then maybe I'd find out what was wrong with me, and I could find a cure. Then I could go back to living free and happy.

But it was all for naught. I just couldn't accept that this was caused by me—my fear and worry. That seemed too easy a solution. I couldn't wrap my head around this for a very long time, and the people who were close to me were growing more and more concerned and confused. If I had taken a few steps back and evaluated what was going on with my mind, I could have started working on the tools that would lead me to freedom from anxiety.

For an overly anxious person, the decision to go to a regular doctor, rather than the ER, is an easy one in moments of crisis. In my experiences with regular doctors, I felt like they just wanted to write out a prescription and send me on my way. It didn't seem like they cared about the root causes of my issues; they only treated the surface symptoms. This led me to seeing a naturopath. A naturopath looks at things in your life that could be contributing to your ailments. They will do a few simple tests to tell you what foods your body will accept and gain benefit from, and what foods your body will reject and might be causing the fatigue that your body is going through. It was the start of a breakthrough for me.

The naturopath found that my body rejects gluten-rich foods. Funny enough, that day I had been reading about how Novak Djokovic (#1 men's tennis player in the world) attributes some of his success to a gluten-free diet. Well, if it was good enough for Novak, it was definitely good enough for me. She also discovered that lemons, almonds, and fruit were all on the list of no-no's for my diet.

I was also told to **cut out** three things completely:

Alcohol—A temporary relief for many suffering from panic and anxiety, alcohol is thought of as a way to relax and calm down, but alcohol causes sugar fluctuations as well as increased lactic acid build-up in the blood, which results in an increase in anxiety, irritability, and disturbed sleep patterns.

Sugar—Sugary foods quickly get absorbed into the bloodstream, which may cause an initial "high" or increase in energy, but soon it wears off as the body increases the production of insulin levels, leaving the person feeling tired and low. The lack of endorphins in the brain, plus the insulin's effect, can result in high amounts of anxiety and depression. The individual might then eat more sugary foods to try to feel better (I know I did), which results in a vicious cycle that can be difficult to stop. It's important to consider the negative effects that sugar might be causing to your mental health the next time you eat sugary foods; it just might put a hold on your recovery, and it's not worth it.

Caffeine—Caffeine works by stimulating the central nervous system. Americans and Europeans rely heavily on their daily coffee, and many studies have found a connection between this addictive stimulant, and the increase of symptoms of anxiety and insomnia. Quitting coffee suddenly can cause withdrawal symptoms such as headache, fatigue, irritability and nervousness, so gradually cutting down the amount you consume, and finding a caffeine-free replacement such as herbal teas, is important.

After cutting out these items from my diet for a few months, the difference in my mood and energy was very noticeable. The naturopath also recommended I **add these foods** to my diet:

Mixed nuts—Did you know that just 1-ounce of walnuts can help replace the stress-depleted B vitamins? Also, cellular damage caused by chronic stress can easily be rebalanced by adding almonds to your diet (I have to avoid almonds, as previously mentioned), which give you a huge boost in vitamin E. Finally, Brazil nuts provide large amounts of zinc, which easily gets drained from high levels of anxiety.

Salmon—Low in mercury and high in omega-3 fatty acids, salmon is rich in vitamin D, which is a well-known mood stabilizer. Studies have shown a connection between low levels of omega-3s and depression, anxiety and attention deficit disorder. Alaskan wild salmon and wild Coho salmon have been found to contain 33% more omega-3s then their farm-raised counterparts due to the differences in diets. If you don't like eating salmon, other great sources of essential omega-3s are flax seed oil, walnut oil, avocados, and organic butter.

Tryptophan-rich foods—Tryptophan is an essential amino acid, which means the body can't manufacture it—it must be taken through diet. Have you ever become sleepy after eating turkey? That's because the tryptophan in turkey is a natural sedative. Tryptophan has been effectively used to treat insomnia—usually 1 to 2 grams of L-tryptophan is enough to induce sleep. The body uses tryptophan to produce niacin and serotonin, which has a positive effect on mood, but in order for tryptophan to be converted into niacin, the body needs enough iron and vitamin B6. Tryptophan-rich foods include eggs, soybeans, cheese, sunflower seeds, turkey, chicken, salmon, beef, milk, bananas, and potatoes.

Blueberries—Blueberries are a super food, and rich in vitamins and plant nutrients, with a variety of antioxidants that are considered to be extremely beneficial for relieving stress. These tiny stress busters are loaded with vitamin C, and help repair and protect cells.

Guacamole—Have a craving for something creamy? Guacamole is loaded with B vitamins commonly known as the stress vitamin, which aids our brain cells and nerves that are lost through continuous stress. Serve it with whole-grain baked chips and your craving for something salty is satisfied.

Complex carbohydrates—Complex carbs are a source of energy that our bodies break down slowly, resulting in a steady stream of energy throughout the day. Complex carbs come in the forms of whole-grain breads and pasta, while simple carbs are things like sugar and cake.

Other complex carbs that should be added to an anti-anxiety diet are fruits (such as oranges, apricots, and pears), vegetables (such as broccoli, spinach, and cucumbers), and legumes (such as kidney beans, soy beans, and pinto beans).

Green tea—Green tea contains L-Theanine, which is involved in the formation of GABA. GABA is a brain chemical that creates the calming and rhythmic electrical impulses in the brain. Despite green tea's caffeine content, which is significantly lower than the levels found in beverages such as coffee, this replacement for coffee drinkers can lead to a huge improvement in mood.

The naturopath then mentioned candida albicans. "Candi wha?" I asked. I had never heard of it, but apparently it was affecting me greatly. She told me that many researchers these days think that anxiety is symptomatic of an overgrowth of candida yeast in the body, and that it is a combination of more than 80 different poisonous toxins. These toxins can mirror and interfere with many of the body's hormones, such as adrenaline, and when this occurs intense feelings of anxiety can be induced.

She then went over a list of symptoms that can be caused by candida overgrowth, and asked me to reply yes or no.

"Foggy mind?" "Yes," I replied.

"Depression or mood swings?" "Yes."

"Panic attacks?" "Yes."

"Poor memory?" "Yes."

"Extreme fatigue?" "YES!"

This gave me a glimmer of hope, and I wanted to follow-up on it to see if the symptoms I was experiencing would subside. So I added certain things to my diet to help detoxify my body:

> **Acidophilus**–Acidophilus helps to maintain a balanced gut flora by helping to keep harmful bacteria under control. It greatly assists in protein digestion, and also produces B vitamins, and has an antibacterial effect that greatly adds to the detoxification of harmful substances.
>
> **Vitamin C**–Vitamin C will allow your immunity to get stronger and overtake the yeast infection faster; a weak immune system makes you more prone to yeast infections.

Coconut oil–In its purest form coconut oil has antimicrobial properties that can help in preventing the spread of yeast infections.

Garlic–Consuming just one clove of garlic daily can be used for treating candida infections as well as other bacterial infections in the body, mainly because of its antiseptic and antibacterial properties.

Ginger–A natural antifungal agent, ginger can be taken by chewing a piece each day or by crushing it and boiling it with a cup of water, and taken as tea up to three times a day.

Water–Two litres of purified water a day is essential to flush out any toxic substances and yeast that are present in the intestines and genital areas.

Diet is one part of anxiety that's often overlooked by sufferers, but it's a very important part that needs to be addressed in order to overcome anxiety. I know that changing these foods and eliminating artificial, fried foods, and preservatives isn't easy. It certainly didn't happen overnight for me. I started with very small changes here and there.

Action Item: Take notice of your diet and pick two foods or stimulants that need to be replaced immediately. How about substituting coffee with herbal teas, and processed snacks with healthy nuts? Begin this change today, and fall in love with how you're no longer searching for short-term band aids, but replacing it with long-term overall health.

I was usually on the tennis court around lunchtime, and I didn't have time to sit and eat so I usually had a large fruit shake. Of course, the sugar in the fruit was harming my body, so I replaced those with veggie shakes—broccoli mixed with lettuce and chia seeds, with honey so it was bearable to drink.

At the beginning, changing my new diet was difficult and filled with cheat days, but as I got used to the foods that helped me eventually conquer anxiety, it became easier. There was just one problem, how would I find the fuel to stay on track and not fall back into my old, self-destructive comfort zone? Like many questions in life, I turned to tennis for the answer.

Trophy Tunnel Vision

When I was a kid, I played in the final of an "under 12" tennis tournament in Vancouver. I was favoured to win these local tournaments because I was playing tennis at a much higher level than the kids in that age group. In the final, I was up against a boy I had beaten before without much resistance, so everything was lined up for another junior tournament victory. As I walked around the tournament site I saw the trophies all perfectly lined up next to each other—one for the winner and one for the finalist. Although the winner's trophy was bigger than the finalist trophy, I wanted the finalist trophy because it was much, much nicer and surrounded in beautiful fake-gold with a carving of someone replicating a tennis serve. I really wanted that trophy. I picked it up. I kissed it. I even walked around with it, as the other players stared at me in confusion.

It was then that I decided to purposely lose the match so I could have that beautiful trophy. I came up with a plan—fake an injury midway through. With the score at 4-4 in the first set, I found the perfect opportunity. I ran for a wide forehand and perfectly rolled over on my ankle, and fell to the ground; the performance would have made any Italian soccer star proud. I winced and mumbled and was told by the physiotherapist who was courtside (damn it!) to take my sock off so she could check the swelling and apply ice to it. She noticed there wasn't any swelling, but I insisted that I needed to be helped off the court and I couldn't continue. I was helped off, and laid on the couch with my leg elevated. I congratulated my opponent while applying the ice to my fake painful ankle.

Once all the finals matches were finished, the trophy presentation began. I patiently waited for the moment when I could take that golden trophy home. I was so excited that for a split second I forgot about my fake injury!

"Dennis Simsek, please come up to the podium and receive your trophy."

I jumped off the couch and confidently walked up to the podium. I shook the hand of the presenter, grabbed my trophy and turned around to give my thanks to the tournament sponsors. I'll never forget the look of utter confusion on their faces. Worst of all, my dad was in the crowd. He knew exactly what I had done. He walked towards me and whispered, "I'll go get the car." That was my signal to get the heck out of that tennis club!

So what did I take from this story that helped keep my diet on track? It's this: Grab hold of something that adds unlimited fuel to your new habit. Whatever, or whomever it is, it must be so powerful that there is no way that anything can stop you from reaching your goal. It's easy to make changes for a few days, then go back to the old habits, but if you draw strength from something that keeps you on track for a long time, the scales are tipped in your favour.

I couldn't stick to a new habit or routine for more than three days, so I drew strength from Robyn and my newborn son, Hayat. You might be wondering, what kind of a name is Hayat? I suggested to Robyn that we name our son Hayat because it means "life" in Turkish. I thought it was a great name to draw great strength on my road to recovery from anxiety. Thankfully, she accepted the name.

Looking back, there were times during my anxiety when I took my family for granted, because my world was all about "me." I was constantly focused on myself; trying not to lose control and allow panic to consume me, but I'd already lost control and didn't even know it.

When your mind is so wired to worry and be anxious, nothing else in the world matters more than tending to the "emergency" that your mind and body perceive. So after a deep crying session, I realized I needed to draw strength from the two people who were counting on me the most. I also wanted to continue on my path to be the best tennis player I could be. Day by day, I drew strength from my family and the sport I loved—that kept me on track to replace my old habits with healthy new ones. Never again would I sit next to Robyn without showing her how much I cared, or go to bed without kissing Hayat good night.

For a few months I was like a man possessed, and although I didn't have a plan on how to change the rest of my negative habits, I did have the strength and motivation to continue my goal of bringing my anxiety levels way down, and living a joyful, abundant life again.

Action Item: What habits are you engaging in that fuel anxiety?

- Write down 2 habits that you want to replace (example: waking up and immediately check emails, or watching TV shows or movies that are over-stimulating and fear-inducing).

- Replace these with two calming things you could be doing instead (example: meditation, yoga, reading, having a cup of tea, etc.).

"Don't expect a different result by doing the same routine," a friend once told me. Through my 6-year battle, I kept hoping that one day my fears and worries would just all go away, but I was engaging in the same old habits.

Me VS Myself

As you pick up new habits and let go of anxiety, you're going to begin to realize that instead of being so tightly knit with your internal self, there's more to life than just you. This realization takes lots of pressure and tension off your shoulders. Once you understand this, you'll find that not only do you have enormous momentum towards your goal, but you're also becoming much more conscious of your surroundings.

Failure was not an option after I committed to change. When things got tough, and I felt like eating the wrong thing or checking-in with my sensations, I'd pull a photo out of my wallet of Robyn and Hayat. Carrying their photos with me, and looking at them, gave me all the strength I needed to take the opposite action. Soon, everything started falling into place.

CHAPTER 13

CHANGE?

**YOU ARE MORE CAPABLE
THAN YOU THINK YOU ARE.**

According to motivational guru Jim Rohn, you are the average of the five people you spend the most time with, so take a good look at who you are surrounding yourself with. It could be making all the difference—good or bad. As I changed, I realized I needed to edit my list of friends, the people I was hanging out with, and the kind of people who I was attracting. Most conversations were negative—complaining about someone or something, which didn't support my goal of conquering anxiety.

And then one glorious day, a small miracle happened. It was at a pro tennis tournament in Turkey. I was in the qualifying draw, playing against someone who was ranked much higher than me. He was also bigger, hit the ball harder, played smarter, and was much younger than me. The only chance I had to win was if he was having a very bad day.

In tennis, it takes 6 games to win a set, and every match is a best 2-out-of-3 sets. Some matches can take a long time and can be very intense battles.

I had had pre-match nerves before, but never quite like this. I was dizzy and I felt a huge anxious lump in my throat (known as globus hystericus). I went to the bathroom 5 or 6 times, surfed the Web to get info on my opponent, sweat through a couple of shirts, and did a warm-up that would match a high-performance training session. I was exhausted, and the match hadn't even started yet!

Grave Thoughts to Brave Thoughts

Most people don't realize how brave and courageous anxiety sufferers, like us, are. Every day we fight for our lives, hoping that in the end we'll survive these awful experiences. So, what I lost in physical energy and stamina I gained in willpower, which was what I needed in order to have a chance. I would fight until the last point to reach my dream as a tennis player—to be professionally ranked on the ATP tour.

I went down quickly, losing the first set 6-2. In the second set, I thought I might have a chance, but I went down again 4-2. That's when things turned around.

A friend of mine started shooting photos and videos of the match. He was doing a documentary about the struggles of being a professional tennis player. For some reason, when my opponent saw him shooting the photos and videos, he started to lose it. The score became 4-3 and I was back in the second set. My opponent asked the referee if my friend would stop snapping photos, but the ref didn't see anything wrong with it.

During the next game my mom showed up to watch the match. My mom always did what she could from the sidelines, in a cute and legal way, for me to win a match, so when she arrived at 4-4 in the second set, I knew I had an even better chance to come back. She cheered for me so loudly that my opponent started to lose it again, and the next thing I knew I won the second set. We went into the third set totally even.

At this point I had built a lot of momentum, and although my friend was done his photo shoot, he kept clicking just to keep my momentum going. More and more people were showing up to watch, and for the first time,

I found myself drawing energy from the crowd, rather than being scared that they were judging me. I had a feeling of invincibility in that third set that I hadn't felt before. Not only was I playing some of the best tennis I'd ever played, I was entertaining the crowd in ways normally not seen in low-level tournaments.

I loved every minute of it, and I didn't want the feeling to end! The final set took 90 minutes. After I won the final point I fell to my knees—the way my tennis idols did—and listened to the roar of the crowd. It was one of the Top 5 greatest moments of my life.

Thinking back on this, I wondered how it happened. After being defeated in the pre-match and first set, how did I not only come back and compete, but also win it in the end? The odds had been against me, but once the match wore on and the crowd started to like me, I felt a very real and positive connection with them.

The power of the mind is amazing. Even when you think you have nothing left physically, your mind can find ways to keep you going. Utilizing the power of your mind—by taking control of your thoughts, and replacing them with new, empowering thoughts—is extremely important. It may be one of the most important tools I used to conquer my anxiety.

But the mind and body are connected, so your physiology is important as well.

Body Language as a Tool

Recall a time when you felt absolutely invincible, like nothing could stop you. What were you thinking? What were you doing? How were you holding your body?

Someone who talks a lot about physiology and body language is Tony Robbins. My dad was a big follower of his. Robbins has said that changing our physiology (our posture, the way we hold ourselves, and the way our body looks) is one way of changing our emotions.

I can vividly remember what my physiology looked like during my memorable tennis match, before, during, and after. My shoulders were pulled back, my chest was pushed out, I was walking tall, and my head was held high. I felt amazing, and my body language reflected that.

When you feel down, what's your body language? Are you slouched, head down, shoulders hunched? That negative posture fuels more unhappiness. It's important to pay attention to your physiology, no matter the situation. This takes time to master, and you may think that it won't matter much, but it made a huge difference in the way I felt. Walk confidently, with your shoulders pulled back and chin up. Sit with your back straight, and speak with confidence until it becomes second nature. Good posture is as important as eating right, exercising, and getting a good night's sleep. I bet you've never heard that before!

Action Item: Your physiology controls your psychology. Begin to take notice of your posture and breathing patterns throughout the day and replace the droopy, unfulfilled look that gives off a low vibration to yourself and the world, and replace it with an empowering posture. Also notice when your breathing is very shallow, and adopt a deep-breathing habit on your inhale and exhale to begin creating balance in your internal environment.

Change Your Focus

Another thing Robbins has talked about to help change the way you feel, is to change your focus. One of his famous sayings is, "Where focus goes, energy flows."

To make his point about focus, he often shares his experience at a race-car driving school with a professional trainer. The trainer, who was in the passenger seat, had a button next to him that would lift the tires and induce a skid, directing the car into the wall. Robbins didn't know when the button would be pushed, and even though he was expecting the skid, when it actually happened, he immediately focused on the wall, which is where he was headed, rather than the track, which is where he wanted to go.

Robbins drove round and round at high speeds, and when the trainer thought Robbins had lost his focus or relaxed a little too much, WHAM, he pushed the button and they headed straight for the wall. Just before they hit the wall, the trainer steered them back in the right direction. This process continued until Robbins figured out why he kept heading for the wall: His focus was on the wall (where he didn't want to go) instead of on the track. As soon as he learned how to override his fear, and natural instinct to focus on the wall, and instead look in the direction of where he wanted to go, he was able to steer in that direction.

An important lesson can be learned from Robbins' experience on the track. If your focus is constantly on what you don't want, then guess what you're going to get more of? What you don't want! **Change your focus to what you *do* want**, but not only when things are easy and your anxiety is at a low level. It's more important to do this when you're in an anxiety-provoking situation. That's when you say to yourself, "I'm not feeling great and my anxiety is rising, but I have a choice: I can focus on trying to stop it quickly (which doesn't work), or focus on the fact that these feelings won't kill me." That way the fear starts to fade and along with the fear, your negative thoughts and bodily sensations with it.

In addition to your focus, are there other areas of your life you'd like to change? For example, your career? Can you make your workplace a more enjoyable place to be? Do you need to build trust with co-workers? Is your work fulfilling? Is it time to switch jobs?

How about your leisure time? Don't you deserve a break once in a while? When was the last time you set aside a day or two to spend on yourself and something you enjoy doing?

What about your education? What can you educate yourself on that interests you?

Taking a deeper look at which aspects of your life need change, then applying a game plan and putting the wheels in motion, is a fulfilling experience that will take you out of your comfort zone, and lead you to face what you fear most, change! Will you run into difficulties? Yes. Will things get more difficult before they get better? Possibly. Will that stop you from following your plan to conquer anxiety? No!

CHAPTER 14

THE LAW OF ATTRACTION

NEUROPLASTICITY: IT IS POSSIBLE TO CHANGE YOUR BRAIN'S ANXIOUS CIRCUITRY.

"I'm home!" Robyn yelled as she walked into our apartment. I was slouched over on the couch exhausted from ruminating about my fear and anxiety. "Hey," I said without much enthusiasm as I quickly turned my attention back to myself and the lump in my throat.

I knew I was bringing Robyn's zest for life way down. She was an optimistic, happy, and caring person, and I confused the hell out of her. First I thought I was dying from a brain tumour, then it was heart disease, then it was a heart attack, and now it was the possibility of throat cancer. I drove her nuts, but she never showed it.

She had brought home a DVD of the movie, "The Secret." I had heard about this video; it was the "thing" at the time, and many people were wondering if it was some kind of a hoax. The premise is that you can have anything you want in life; anything at all, and that we have the ability to manifest our dreams by the power of thought. The law of attraction states that our thoughts have a vibration, and it's being acted on every moment; this creates our reality.

Robyn thought watching the video might help me overcome my anxiety disorder. I read the back of the DVD and thought it was a bunch of baloney! But maybe there was a grain of truth in it that would help me. I was desperate.

Looking for a Solution

As I watched The Secret, I saw a boy who wanted a bike, and a few days later it showed up on his doorstep; a guy who expected cheques to appear in his mailbox and eventually they appeared; and a genie came out of a lamp and told a guy he had unlimited wishes; etc.

At that point in my life I had a steady career teaching tennis, and a few good friends who I gave great advice to when they needed it. I told my tennis students that they could become anything they wanted to be. I was good at coming up with solutions for other people, but I had no solution for myself. I was severely depressed, and I feared everything, from driving to walking too fast, in case I had a panic attack, or worse. It was a strange time; I needed to look at what was going on in my life in order to transform myself into who I wanted to become.

What I took from The Secret is that the law of attraction brings similar things together, and our thoughts and mental images create our reality. That scared the crap out of me! All I ever thought about was how I was going to die from the symptoms of fear. Did this mean I was nearing death?

When you present this kind of a movie or book to someone suffering from anxiety, you have to understand a couple of things. First, we anxious people are desperate for a cure and will do anything to get rid of what we're going through. Second, although we want a quick fix, we don't have the patience to "recondition" our minds and change our lives. (I later realised that this was the only way to the cure I was searching for.) Third, we will try ANYTHING once, and then quickly label it as "helped a bit," and

"I might continue with it as long as it provides me with consistent relief," or "It sucks, and no one should try it."

So of course I had to at least try it. The Secret has three major steps to follow in order to manifest what you want. 1) Ask for what you want. 2) Believe that you already have what it is you've asked for. 3) Imagine what it would feel like if you already had what you asked for.

After the movie was released, many of my friends hopped on the law-of-attraction bandwagon and became strangely upbeat. One of them, Kim, had a weight issue and must have been 80 pounds overweight. She had tried diets, working out with trainers, and even went to fat camp! Nothing seemed to help, but she also never stuck with anything long enough for it to work. She had seen the movie 9 times, and even had a shirt with The Secret plastered on it. I didn't need to ask Kim what she thought of the movie—she was beaming with a newfound attitude. She told me she did the three steps day and night for a few weeks, and felt like she had lost weight. I had to have a talk with her.

"Kim," I said as we sat down to have a cup of tea at the park, "you're not losing weight, sweetie, in fact I think you may have gained some weight."

I burst her bubble and felt awful about it at the time, but I had to say it. There aren't any shortcuts to losing weight and getting fit. She was living in a world of delusion and I had to get her back on track. Her diet was awful, she rarely exercised, and even drove her car to the grocery store, which was only one block away from where she lived. After that day, Kim wouldn't talk to me because of how harsh I was to her; I lost a good friend.

A lot of what The Secret professes is time-tested psychological tricks that help keep a person motivated, which I thought was pretty cool, but I had to look deeper to see how it could help me overcome my own battle. I needed more proof of the law of attraction. At the time, many celebrities attributed a lot of their success to the law of attraction, so it definitely got me thinking, and some proof was right under my nose.

I realised a few things about myself after watching the movie: I was very negative and didn't get much joy out of life; I was a victim of my lack of awareness about the law of attraction in my own life; and I recognised that my recurring thoughts did lead to the actions I took.

I quickly started to apply what I learned. First I stopped watching crime shows and scary movies. Then I started filtering out words—I completely eliminated "can't," "scared," "panic," "what if," "tired," "depressed," "fatigue," and so on. This action actually made a big difference in my mood. I also strapped an elastic band to my wrist and any time I thought or said one of the words on my "no-no" list, I immediately snapped the elastic. This created a painful connection in my mind between the thought and the pain I was feeling; it was great!

Sharp Shooter

In considering Step 2—believe that you've already received what you want—it reminded me of a time during my early high school. My dad thought it would be a good idea for me to be involved in different sports when I wasn't training on the court. I joined the soccer team, the baseball team, and the basketball team. I loved all of these, but basketball stood out much more than the others. I wanted to become a better basketball player, but I sucked at shooting. I was faster then everyone, jumped as high as everyone else, and understood the basketball playbook very well, but I sucked at shooting.

My basketball coach used me to distribute the ball, and to set picks, etc., but I wanted to be a bigger part of the team's offence. He wouldn't let me unless I learned how to shoot better.

For the next few weeks I pulled a Michael Jordan; I was in the gym every morning before tennis and every evening after tennis. I must have shot a thousand shots per day from every area of the court, but I was only getting a little better. Something was missing.

Then came a rare moment of softness from my dad. He stepped onto the basketball court and started shooting free throws with me. My dad never played basketball in his life. He grabbed the ball and tried to dribble it to the free throw line with no success. Then he just walked the ball there. He put his left foot in front of his right foot, just behind the free throw line, and told me not to talk to him until he said it was OK.

He held the ball up as if he was holding a giant egg, with two hands right next to each other behind the ball. I almost started to crack up at how funny he looked. He stared at the rim for 10 seconds and told me, "Pass the ball to me after each shot, please." Wow! He said please!

He let the shot go off of his fingertips and with one of the ugliest follow-throughs I've ever seen, the ball went straight into the hoop for a swish without touching any part of the rim or backboard. I passed the ball back to him, and he looked at the rim again for 10 seconds before taking his shot, and again—swish.

I thought, what luck! So I passed him the ball again, and for a third straight time—swish! Then again, and again. Here I was, practicing day and night and get absolutely no results, and my old man jumps in out of nowhere and nails 5 free throws like it was nothing. He started to look at the rim less and less after the first 5, and he made the next 23 shots without touching the rim. By the end of it he was only taking around 2 seconds to shoot the ball.

After the free throw session I asked him how he was able to make 28 free throws in a row without hitting the rim having never shot a basketball before. "Visualise and focus," he said calmly. He showed me how to create a mental image of how I wanted the ball to go in the net after each shot, and to be able to do it in a split second. Because of his teaching I was able to be a big part of the offence on my team because I had become a "sharpshooter."

As sceptical as I was when I first heard about the law of attraction, I took some of the pieces from the movie and used it to recover from my anxiety disorder and also to lift my tennis-playing career to new heights.

Don't be at the mercy of events or circumstances, or even other people. Understand that you are the cause, just as I was, and your reality is the effect. The sooner you realise this, the sooner your life will turn around.

CHAPTER 15

BOUND FOR BALI

**RECOGNIZE WHAT YOU DO HAVE
CONTROL OVER, AND WHAT YOU DON'T.**

Have you ever thought about turning your whole world around and doing something totally different? Like move your newly engaged partner and newborn baby to Bali, maybe? That's the idea that came to me, and I acted on it.

My doctor had been suggesting I take a vacation, or change my worldview in some way, which got me thinking about possibly leaving Canada—and my steady career, nice home, and amazing friends. At the same time, a job opportunity came to me through my good friend, Henri, to coach tennis at a resort and compete in local money tournaments around Asia.

Henri was living in Singapore; he was a Buddhist, a deejay, and one of the most carefree guys I'd ever met. It seemed like nothing ever bothered him; his optimism was amazing. I wanted to be just like him. He told me how beautiful Bali was—he'd been traveling back and forth between Bali and

Singapore at the time. Carefree was definitely the life I needed. So I did some research, and accepted the tennis coach offer and signed a one-year contract.

Then it was time to move. We proceeded to do what every Canadian does—have a garage sale. Sadly, we had to give our dog away. We put an ad in the local classifieds and within three days a wonderful family came and took our beautiful black lab, Binny, to her new home. I'll never forget Robyn crying that entire night.

Was I being selfish? Absolutely. I wanted to move to Bali because my GAD and panic attacks were completely controlling me; I thought maybe I could find some natural ways to combat my anxiety over there, and a change of scenery might turn everything around for me. I was sure I could get my life back, and become the future husband and father I needed to be.

I decided to fly to Bali first, before Robyn Hayat, so I could find a nice place for us to live. We bought our plane tickets; I got on the plane, and headed off just three weeks after our decision to move. I felt butterflies in my stomach as I got on the plane; I didn't know what to expect from this adventure since I'd never been to that part of the world, but I wanted to make sure that everything went smoothly, and finally be done with my anxiety.

A New World

I landed at the airport in Bali and met the director of the tennis section for all the resorts there. He was a very nice guy, and he made me feel incredibly relaxed. My most valuable luggage—three tennis racquets and my bag—were then tied to the top of his tiny car and we were off. The car was filled with all sorts of mini tennis nets and racquets for kids, so every pot hole on the road (there are a lot in Bali) made me cringe because I knew my racquets were feeling the effects up on the roof.

We finally made our way to the small house where I'd be staying temporarily. Five other coaches lived in the house, and I immediately bonded with all of them. They told me to get ready for the night. They were headed to a place called Kuta, where the nightlife was incredible and the beaches were beautiful. As tired as I was, I had to see it for myself, so I unpacked and got ready to go just 30 minutes after I had arrived.

While unpacking, I realised that two of my new tennis racquets were broken. I wasn't sure if it was from the plane trip or the car ride, either way it made me sad because the relationship between a player and his racquets is tighter than anything else, and I couldn't afford new ones! Sad as I was, I got in our van.

The team offered me a beer as we made our way towards Kuta. I accepted it, even though I knew how alcohol raised my adrenaline levels the next day, and always put me through unbearable physical symptoms that led to full-on panic attacks. Three beers later, and some rowdiness in the van, we made it to Kuta. At this point I was so tired I could barely feel my legs, but continued on to the first nightclub on the beach strip. I looked around before we went in and I couldn't believe how beautiful everything was. I was just sad I couldn't really enjoy it much at that point.

I did the best I could to remain upbeat even though I had jet lag and the time change between Canada and Bali was taking its toll. The energy in the club was incredible—the music was loud, laser lights flashed everywhere and clothing was optional. Wow, people in Kuta really knew how to party! We got to the bar and my new roommates ordered me a triple gin and tonic. I knew if I had that drink it would be the end of me that night, and it surely was.

I was missing my family so much that all I wanted to do was find a place to relax and collect myself. I walked across the street and lied down on a bench; the rest was history, it was lights out. The next day I was awakened by a dancing monkey and his trainer, who were the main attraction in Kuta at the time, and somehow I was smack in the centre of the beach.

Questions ensued: How did I get all the way to the middle of the beach? Where did my team go? What time was it? Most importantly, where the hell am I? I slowly started to get up and look around. Fear overtook my thoughts, not because I was lost, but because I knew I had drank the night before, and the combination of that and my tiredness was a recipe for disaster. My short-term memory was better than my long-term memory, so I hailed a taxi and told the driver to head for the airport; from there I thought I could guide him to the house. The drive from the airport the night before wasn't that long, so I thought I had a chance to find my place fairly easily from there. That was not the case.

We drove around what seemed like the whole island, and somehow after two hours of asking people directions and driving some more, we ran into the place I was staying. YES!

"120000 Rupiah," the driver said, which I knew was somewhere in the $12 range. I thought, wow what a deal! I went to grab my wallet from my pocket and realised it wasn't there! I frantically looked around the taxi, on the ground, under the seats, in my back pocket, nothing. I had either lost it or completely forgotten to take it with me.

I checked to see if anyone was home, so I could look for my wallet or ask for a loan, but no one was there. I negotiated with the driver and eventually got his address, which was very close to where I was staying, and promised I'd deliver the money I owed him by the end of the day, he thankfully agreed. There was one more thing I had to deal with—the fact that my house key was in my missing wallet.

As I sat outside the front door waiting for my roommates to come back, I remembered that there was a pool in the backyard, so I made the best of the situation and went for a swim. Afterward, I took a nap on the grass. As night approached, I heard someone calling my name.

"Dennis!" My roommates were home after a day of training and teaching tennis to the resort guests. They told me how their legendary night went, and said they couldn't find me anywhere so they thought I'd gone home. I snapped back, "I didn't know where home was!"

After getting all pissy and storming off, I collected myself, found my wallet, paid back the taxi driver, and apologized to my roommates later on that evening. This was just a rough start, right? I said goodnight to everyone and dozed off, hoping for better days ahead.

Over the next few weeks, I got into a nice rhythm with my training, teaching, and friendships. Things were good, but I was still struggling to find a respectable place for us to live that was near work, and I only had three days until Robyn and Hayat arrived. Thankfully, my boss introduced me to an agent in Bali who showed me a few places. Housing prices in Nusa Dua, a resort area in southern Bali, were too high, so I settled on a place 15 minutes from work. It was a nice three-bedroom home and I was excited for Robyn and Hayat to arrive and move in. I packed up my stuff, said goodbye to my roommates, and took off.

I also rented a Jeep—if you can call it that. This thing had no seatbelts, had a standard transmission (I'd never driven standard in my life), and the driver's seat was on the left side, just like the roads. I stalled about 18 times on my way home from the car rental place.

During the next few days I got better and better at driving. Then the day came to pick up Robyn and Hayat at the airport. What a great day that was. We made our way to the parking lot, but there was a problem—I forgot to get a baby seat for the Jeep. With Robyn holding Hayat in her lap, I drove at a snail's pace and safely made it home, but not before I got an earful from her on the way. We parked the Jeep outside our new place and regrouped.

As I flung open the front door with great joy, and we went in to our new home, Robyn quickly noticed something in the bedroom. "Dennis? Did you know about this?" she asked.

There were two lizards crawling on the back wall, four cockroaches scampering around the floor, and a cat lying on our bed. I freaked out, grabbed Robyn and Hayat, and slammed the bedroom door shut. When I had signed the contract, I hadn't paid attention to how open the house was to the outside—the bedroom had a small opening all around, so anything the size of a cat could easily get in, the living room had a barred door to the outside but had gaps in it as well, and the second and third bedrooms had openings on the ceilings with no way of closing them. This was different for us, to say the least. I immediately called the landlord, and he told me that other than the cockroaches, the lizards and the visiting cat were normal.

"WHAT?" I yelled. "You want us to sleep with a lizard and cats running around our house? Why didn't you tell me about these wonderful creatures?" "You never asked," he replied.

I swiftly contacted a team of cockroach killers who came over and took care of the situation. I couldn't believe the size of these cockroaches—they were as big as my hand!

"Welcome to Bali, Honey," I said to Robyn, but she wasn't impressed. I had a lot of work to do to make it up to her.

It took us a few months to adjust to life in Bali, and we did miss some of the conveniences we had in Canada, such as a bathtub, and a house without

animals crawling on the walls (we named the two lizards Ben and Jerry). I still struggled with panic attacks,

health anxiety, and hypochondria from time to time, but nowhere near what I'd been going through back in Canada. Being in Bali distracted me from my anxiety disorder, and myself, and put my attention onto other things. Work was very fulfilling; I was introducing tennis to kids who would never have been able to afford a racquet, and they loved it. We were also doing things as a family, like visiting places and learning about the culture, and I picked up a hobby that helped me with my mental health more than anything—photography.

Photography as a Mental Health Tool

You may be thinking, why photography? I think photography is the BEST hobby for an anxious person. Photography opens up your outside world and takes the attention off your inner world—worries about physical symptoms, fatigue, deadlines, bills, etc. When my conscious mind was on the lookout for beautiful places and things in Bali, I started to see things in the outside world that I had never noticed before.

If you don't believe, me give it a shot! Grab a camera and head outside, and see how creative you can be. See something that catches your attention and start snapping photos. You may find that you start to see small details in your photos that you may never have seen before.

Tennis in Bali

Since tennis in Indonesia was pretty nonexistent, I won most of the tennis tournaments there, and was treated like Roger Federer most of the time. The joy that people in Bali get from the simplest things—such as a soccer ball, or a tennis racquet—are things we take for granted in the Western world. Their

idea of a soccer ball is a bunch of old newspapers glued together and hardened. But even with the lack of proper coaches, a decent tennis court, or proper equipment, once I put the small tennis racquets into the hands of the Balinese kids, their enthusiasm fuelled the way to learn certain skills quickly, and to my amazement most of them were rallying at a short court distance quicker than the kids back home in Canada. These kids also listened to their coach, took good care of their racquets, and respectfully communicated with each other.

The trip brought us lots of great memories, and I really enjoyed the kindness of the people in Bali.

When my doctor told me I needed a change of pace and a vacation, I never thought we'd move to Bali, but somehow it happened and it was great advice. Does this mean that you must move out of your country to find peace and release from anxiety? No, it's the lifestyle changes, which can be made anywhere, that alter our belief systems.

However, I must admit that seeing things in a different light really helped to turn my life around from constantly thinking about me, me, me, to helping others, which positively affects our own lives more than we know. As mentioned, everything starts with a decision. Becoming fed-up with how a certain aspect of your life is going is the first step, after that, finding your way is easy because the road is already paved.

Action Item: Make a list of the things that are creating negativity within you, and ask yourself how much control you have over those things. You can't control people, the weather, or other drivers, so if these are on your list, it's time to gain some clarity over them and begin changing your perspectives.

CHAPTER 16

AN INSPIRATION? REALLY?

**BECOME THE SUCCESS STORY THAT
INSPIRES OTHER TO FACE THEIR FEARS.**

At the age of 32, when most tennis pros are thinking about retiring, I was playing some of the best tennis ever. Since my mind was clearer, and I didn't fear panic attacks, I decided it was time to give my life-long goal of getting a professional tennis ranking another shot. Although I had won that dramatic match described earlier, I lost the match the next day, which denied me the ATP point that I needed so badly. Winnipeg, Canada, was the place I had my sights on in search of that elusive point. I was looking for a tournament that would potentially have a weak qualifying draw (the matches needed to win to be able to play in the main tournament). I arrived in Winnipeg and checked into a local hostel, excited to get to the tournament site and hit the practice courts. As I practiced with some of the younger players, I realised that the overall level of pro tournaments had risen significantly from 10 years ago.

As the movie character Rocky Balboa said, "The world ain't all sunshine and rainbows. It's a very mean and nasty place, and I don't care how tough you are, it will beat you to your knees and keep you there permanently if you let it. You, me, or nobody is gonna hit as hard as life. But it ain't about how hard you hit. It's about how hard you can get hit and keep moving forward; how much you can take and keep moving forward. That's how winning is done!"

I refused to lose that match, even though by the end I physically had nothing left. My mind wouldn't let my body give up because I had a relentless drive to win. If you don't have this kind of determination to conquer your fear and anxiety, you'll be living with panic and anxiety forever. It will literally suck the energy, happiness, and life right out of you.

The tournament ended well for me—I accomplished my goal of achieving a professional tennis ranking and could then call myself a legitimate professional tennis player!

Becoming an Inspiration

Towards the end of my GAD and panic disorder, I started sharing what I had gone through with quite a few people. Even so, I was surprised when I returned home from Winnipeg and heard people using the word "inspiration" when referring to me. They realized how I had moved from an all-time low of severe depression and thinking about taking my own life, to overcoming those obstacles and actually inspiring others in the process. What a transformation!

Everyone loves a success story that provides hope, and so I found myself becoming a role model for people who were fighting the same battles I had. Instead of inflating my ego—as it would have in the past—I realized I could help other anxiety sufferers, and at the same time maintain my own recovery by hearing success stories.

I remember one woman who I'd kept in contact with over the years. I knew she was going through a tough time, and since we lived in the same city, we met one day to talk. Doctors had advised her to go home and rest for a while; maybe take a vacation. She said those suggestions weren't working, and she wasn't able to feel anything toward her friends and loved ones anymore. This was draining her energy and limiting her life.

I knew from my experience, that she needed to loosen her attitude toward herself, and lose the fear that surrounded her every move. Then she could get back on the track to rekindling her relationships. I told her this was something that would naturally happen over time.

One of the exercises we used to bring her back into the present moment, and to ground her, was to look around and notice four different objects that were around her that she could see; four sounds that she could hear; and four things that she could feel. This is an excellent exercise that will help anyone get back to being in the moment rather than worrying about the past or what might happen in the future. She used this exercise whenever her mind wandered and her anxiety symptoms escalated.

By working on being in the present moment, this woman eventually recovered and returned to the person she once was. Her family was thrilled! Of course it didn't happen overnight—she had to put a lot of work into the exercises she did. She also learned the art of letting go when she thought someone looked at her funny or said something critical. She gained incredible momentum just by learning to let go and be present.

Action Item: Brainstorm ideas on how you can be an inspiration to others. You've probably got an amazing skill that you're hiding from the world. How about sharing or teaching that skill in some way? Maybe you could start a group? Create an online class? Anything to begin tapping into an audience that is ready to listen to your teaching.

CHAPTER 17

THE 6 STEPS TO FREEDOM

MASTER PATIENCE IN YOUR ANXIETY RECOVERY, AND YOU MASTER EVERYTHING ELSE.

After 6 years of suffering, I can say for certain that there's no such thing as a magic pill to overcome panic and anxiety. It takes patience and time, and it's not easy. I approached my recovery like a scientist trying to discover the perfect formula. I was determined to find my own formula for overcoming extreme levels of anxiety and panic attacks, and I am proud to say that I was successful! It gave me back my life, and if you're suffering the way I was, it can do the same for you if you understand and apply the following steps.

Step 1: Complete Acceptance—For people struggling with GAD, learning to accept that they have an anxiety disorder, and nothing more, can be highly therapeutic on its own. It's also helpful to accept the temporary discomfort and symptoms that come with anxiety. Instead of thinking about a potential health concern you might have, acceptance of your anxiety means that you understand that what you are experiencing is only a reaction to self-generated fear.

Step 2: Become Knowledgeable—It's vitally important that acceptance is followed by education. Learn about how and why panic attacks happen and what GAD is. Knowledge is a powerful tool that will give you deeper understanding and help to build your self-confidence.

Step 3: Build on Facts—Building on the facts means fully understanding that a panic attack is uncomfortable, but it has never hurt anyone or has contributed to poor health in the future. Building on the facts also means looking at your past and truly knowing that what you fear most has not come true, and it most likely never will. It means replaying the mental images of those times in the past when you successfully let the storm of panic pass, even though you may have thought you were doomed. So much energy and attention is given to our fears; we give them too much respect. Some people carry small cards with them to remind them of the facts about their worries. Build on your own facts and reap the rewards.

Step 4: Take Action—The following quote, by Johann Wolfgang von Goethe, turned my life around: "Knowing is not enough; we must apply. Willing is not enough; we must do." Life can and will be the way you want it to be again…even better, but no one has achieved any goal without taking action and applying knowledge. Start by recognizing your small achievements, which will build your confidence, lift your spirits and begin to bring you much-needed peace. Taking action requires a big step out of your comfort zone, so be prepared to get comfortable with being uncomfortable for the time being. And don't get discouraged if you don't see results in the first few days or weeks—that's not uncommon. What's important is that you commit to your recovery, and stay the course.

Step 5: Accept Setbacks—Everyone who suffers from an anxiety disorder recovers at their own pace. When you experience a setback, whether it's recurring fearful thoughts, panic attacks or anything else, anxiety is doing all it can to stand its ground because it's confused by your new mindset and actions. For example, if I tried skateboarding at this point in my life, I'd be absolutely awful at it. I could either quit trying or persevere. If I stuck with it, in time my newfound hobby would become easy, natural, and effortless. Setbacks are normal, and should be expected and accepted; they are practically guaranteed. **Remember that two steps forward and one step back is still progress!** Don't get frustrated and lose hope. Be gentle on yourself, let your recovery come in time, and don't force it.

Step 6: Practice Patience—The key ingredient that puts everything together is patience. Impatience is the result of being dissatisfied with slow progress. It's easy to feel overwhelmed and then lose the motivation to keep on the path of change, but stay the course and move forward. Let time pass, and practice patience no matter how many setbacks occur during your recovery. Continue to remind yourself of the benefits of overcoming your current condition and use it to add fuel to your patience. No one can predict when you will fully desensitize yourself from your fears, but as long as you're facing in the right direction, all you have to do is keep moving forward.

Action Item: Understand the 6 steps to overcoming GAD and recognize which steps you need to work on. Once you pinpoint those areas that need work, put together a plan of how to begin changing your mindset, or begin taking action in that direction starting today.

A Sense of Gratitude

In my opinion, anyone who is going through an anxiety disorder—or even just a rough patch—should take time to visit or help people who are worse off than they are. The act of selflessness builds a sense of gratitude in the giver and the receiver.

As I was working on step #6 in my recovery, I did something I never thought I'd do: I called a children's hospital and asked if I could volunteer there for a few hours a week. I wanted to step into the world of other people who were suffering with the very real health problems that I was afraid of. I realized that although I was living a nightmare, it was a nightmare I created and sustained; one that could be turned around by applying these 6 steps.

Since it took lots of self-discipline to play professional level tennis, I figured I already had an important tool in my arsenal to overcome anxiety as well.

As I was escorted through the halls of the hospital, I prepared myself to meet these brave kids who were ACTUALLY fighting for their lives, and with it making sure that I was in a peak state so that I could add as much as I could to their lives. As I entered the room, I saw the faces of some of the happiest kids I had ever seen! It was incredible to witness them mingling with each other and teaching each other different things. The energy in the room was amazing. For those few hours, nothing was about me, it was all about them, and I loved it! During that time, being around those brave children, if you had asked me if I had an anxiety disorder, I wouldn't have had any idea what you were talking about.

I had brought a few small tennis racquets for the kids, and they loved it, swinging away as they learned what forehands and backhands were. They didn't need to say anything—I knew by looking in their eyes how grateful they were. I left the racquets, tennis balls, and some tennis clothes and said my goodbyes, and sadly left. What an incredible connection I had made with these kids. Leaving the hospital, a feeling of frustration welled up inside me. I couldn't believe how selfish I had been for those 6 years of GAD and panic—everything was about me, me, me, and how I was feeling, what was threatening me, where I needed to be, what pleased me. I was disgusted, to say the least. I made a decision that day, that I would never be so selfish again. I dedicated myself to helping others overcome their mental health issues, as well as helping people who were not as well off as me in other aspects of life.

Recovery Time

It took me about 9 months to conquer my anxiety after suffering for nearly 6 years. Everyone recovers at a different speed, depending on their level of anxiety and how long they've been suffering. So when you hear about someone who got their life back in one month, and you're on the third month, don't get discouraged. Success could be right around the corner.

How will you know when you have fully recovered?

- When your body has had enough rest and nourishment that your energy is back and chronic fatigue is no longer an issue.

- When a fearful thought (which may continue to creep in) doesn't send you into an anxious cycle, and you can brush it off knowing it's just another false alarm.

- When you stop giving attention to those false alarms, then anxiety will recede.

- When you stop trying to *think* positive, and hoping that this alone will turn things around. Action is what will turn your anxiety disorder around. I was the most anxious positive person ever. I told myself lies such as things are getting better. THINGS WERE NOT GETTING BETTER! Telling yourself the truth will get you to take action.

- When you start taking responsibility for your anxiety disorder. Certain factors such as your childhood may actually be a reason for the anxiety you're currently experiencing, but once you begin to take responsibility for your issues you stop playing the blame game and stop being a victim. Once you take the power back into your own hands, you will begin to recognize that you ALWAYS have a choice in the matter, it just takes time to recondition yourself until desensitization begins.

- When your thoughts, emotions and physical body are in sync. It may seem that at the moment your thoughts are out of control, you're emotionally unstable, and you feel completely fatigued. Once these three things are in alignment, you won't have to struggle to have clear thoughts, feel balanced and have your energy back. Days will feel enjoyable and easy for you again.

CHAPTER 18

LIFE AFTER ANXIETY

**THE GREAT THING ABOUT FEAR IS THAT
WHEN YOU RUN TOWARDS IT, IT RUNS AWAY.**

Time is all you have in life, and once your time is up you don't want to be looking back on your life wondering why you didn't start taking steps sooner to end your anxiety, or anything else that might be contributing to your negativity. During the lowest point in my life, I was only moments from taking my life while I sat in my car completely drunk. I just couldn't take any more and I had no control over myself. Up to that point, I had had suicidal thoughts but I never shared them with my therapist because I thought she might find a way to lock me up!

The reason I didn't run my car over a bridge that night was because I didn't want to be so selfish and leave my family in pain, and have my son grow up without his dad. As much as I wanted to wake up the next day and become interested in life again, I realised that it doesn't work that way with depression and anxiety. My anxiety disorder had developed slowly over time due to personal disappointments and problems that led to fear and pessimism.

On the tennis court I noticed a few things change during my recovery. One was that I got butterflies in my stomach again, which is a normal feeling a lot of athletes have before a competition. I accepted this as a huge step in my recovery because it replaced the other pre-match anxious routines I used to go through like multiple washroom trips, and the trembling in my hands and legs. I learned that a little fear before a tennis match was a good thing.

A Learning Experience

Our thoughts really do create our reality and in time I realised that my failures were only lessons. When I began to see those failures as feedback, rather than using them to self-destruct, I was able to turn everything around and get my life back. There was an event in Singapore that I was invited to, it was  a weekend of amazing tennis highlighted by the legends of tennis: Ilie Nastase, Henri Leconte, Mansour Bahrami, Paul Harhuis and Jacco Eltingh. I was invited to a dinner the night before the exhibitions, and I got to sit right next to Ilie Nastase! It felt surreal. He was the #1 tennis player in the world back in the day and now is an amazing tennis entertainer who travels the world and does these kinds of exhibitions. I took the opportunity to be a pest and ask Ilie a few questions. As the conversation flowed, he said, "You sure know a lot about my life, don't you?" I told him I did my homework and how grateful I was to be sitting next to him. Later on he mentioned what a pleasure it was for him to chat with such an interesting character—ME!

Me VS Myself

During my anxiety disorder I wouldn't have had the guts to say one word to Ilie, but everything had changed and my confidence had returned.

During that weekend I saw someone at the event who looked familiar; it was my old friend Lucas from Bali. What a small world. We caught up on how our lives were going. Lucas noticed that I had become a completely different, and he couldn't understand how I had changed so much for the better. I told him my story and he listened intently. I shared with him that although I still fear things from time to time I don't let those fears dictate how I live my life, and that it took me way too long to turn my mindset around.

The weekend was highlighted by the fact that Lucas and I were asked to play a doubles exhibition against a former #1 doubles team in the world: Paul Haarhuis and Jacco Eltingh.

They were larger than life to me, and I'll always remember watching them play when I was a kid. Lucas and I quickly went up 2 games to 0 on the slippery grass courts. I looked at the faces of my opponents and could see they were worried since the crowd had come to see them play and here were a couple of tennis journeymen beating them and making it look easy. I felt that it would have been a disaster for the weekend event if we did beat them, so we decided to play more to the crowd then try to beat these legends.

We quickly found out how good they were once they started hitting shots I'd never seen before. In one game, Eltingh had hit 3 shots over 3 different points that bounced on our side of the court and spun back to theirs. "Truly legendary status," I thought to myself.

The exhibition brought in a few hundred people and we put on an incredible show for everyone. Eventually we lost, but I left the court thinking that it had been one of the most enjoyable matches I had ever played in my life. Paul later asked me why I never made it to a higher level in tennis. I told him I lost sight of what lifted me up and focused too much on what brought me down. The weekend went flying by and I learned a lot from those legends; I couldn't believe at their age how much passion they still had for the game. They loved it.

The Anxiety Guy Tells All

Closure

Fifteen years after my father left my mom and me, I started to rebuild my relationship with him. I had lots of questions for him, but one stood out more than any other: "Why were you so hard on me in tennis, but nothing

else?" He really couldn't answer that, and I noticed some shame in his body language. I believe that if he could go back in time he would redo certain things that affected his relationship with my mother and me. I knew I had to forgive him—in the end, he is my

father and he did apologize for the way he was, even though he didn't give me a deeper reason as to why. I felt an unbelievable sense of relief after our chat—the kind of relief you feel after accomplishing a long-term goal.

I used to nickname my father "the beast," because he was like a scary beast during my childhood. If anyone asked about my father, I told him or her

to refer to him as just "the beast." Crazy, over-the-top tennis dads are common in tennis—it wasn't surprising to see two dads going at each other in a verbal battle in junior tournaments across North America.

Many of the pro players who had father issues over tennis never got a chance to "start over" with them, but I was glad I did. The worst feeling is having something lingering inside of you that you want an answer for. After our chat, we started to bond again and he would tell me how life was in Turkey. No one loves their country as much as my father does, and with how the country was excelling combined with its beauty, I couldn't blame him.

It pains me to see other people suffering from GAD, panic attacks, and depression because I know what they're going through. It may have first started because of the pressure to "fit in," or a feeling in your body that felt odd, or scary, or a recurring traumatic event that became difficult to forget. To those people I say you can grow stronger from this pain if you don't let it destroy you. I am living proof to everyone that the true way to success through an anxiety disorder, or a sport you truly love, is to always try just one more time, because the past can't hurt you anymore, unless you let it.

At the end of your life, I want you to be able to look back and marvel at the way you handled your anxiety disorder. I don't want you to look back and think "what if?" This path you are heading down may be unfamiliar and uncomfortable, but it is the path that you must take. Take it now, take your life back, and begin giving others permission to face their own fears through your actions. They will realize through your success that they have a choice that will lead them on the path to recovery from their anxiety disorder.

CHAPTER 19

THE SECOND COMING OF BALI

THE SECRET TO CHANGE IS TO FOCUS ALL OF YOUR ENERGY ON BUILDING THE NEW, NOT FIGHTING THE OLD.

Five years after my first catastrophic adventures in Bali dealing with overwhelming anxiety, I found myself wanting…wanting to go back to Bali, Indonesia, and once and for all change the associations and pairings I had

created in this beautiful land. I made up my mind, discussed it with Robyn and Hayat, and we decided to embark on the journey of a lifetime.

I needed to come up with other reasons for why we should go to Bali, so I created one-day workshops, and anxiety retreats, for people in Asia and Europe to come see me there and transform their lives in a short time. It was set up perfectly to kill two birds with one stone for me, and off we went.

As I approached the exact environments in Bali where I previously had I thought my life would end, due to intense panic and anxiety, I realized that the pairings between this place causing increased sensitivity within me

had been replaced with a feeling of empowerment. With each and every area I revisited in Bali, the stronger this feeling became, and the more confused I felt.

Through a combination of CBT and NLP I learned that to change the pairing between a situation and the connection to anxiety, you have to revisit the area and allow new neurons to fire together and wire together as the associations changed. As much truth as this holds for so many people, I learned that momentum and progress is the ultimate winner.

When you consistently reprogram your mind through new thought patterns, words, behaviours, and imagination, the new programming affects all areas of your life.

The old patterns of health anxiety, GAD, and panic never arose in Bali; I was too deep in rapport with this new me. I loved it. I expected it. And living life at this level was what I deserved. I learned that at the deepest level when you replace who you think you are and your self image, it affects everything. It affects how you see yourself, the world, and your future. That's why identity is everything.

Now that you've become more knowledgeable about your condition, you're ready to turn your life around through a proven CBT based method I've created through my extensive research as well as seeing what has consistently worked for the warriors I've personally worked with over the years, the End The Anxiety Program (located at www.anxietyexit.com). I look forward to hearing about your future success stories.

Lightning Source UK Ltd.
Milton Keynes UK
UKHW020816220120
357404UK00009B/109